TENNIS
and the Mind

Books by Barry Tarshis

TENNIS AND THE MIND 1977
WHAT IT COSTS 1977
THE STEADY GAME (*with Manuel Orantes*) 1977
SIX WEEKS TO A BETTER LEVEL OF TENNIS 1977
TENNIS FOR THE BLOODY FUN OF IT
(*with Rod Laver and Roy Emerson*) 1976
THE CREATIVE NEW YORKER 1973
THE ASPHALT ATHLETE 1972
JULIE HARRIS TALKS TO YOUNG ACTORS
(*with Julie Harris*) 1971

TENNIS
and the Mind

BARRY TARSHIS

A Tennis *Magazine Book*

ATHENEUM / SMI   NEW YORK

1977

Library of Congress Cataloging in Publication Data

Tarshis, Barry.
  Tennis and the mind.
    1. Tennis—Psychological aspects. I. Title.
GV1002.9.P75T37   1977   796.34'2'09   77–76789
ISBN 0–689–10749–8

Acknowledgements

This book could never have been written without the help of a great many people.

I am indebted, first of all, to all of the professional players and coaches whose comments appear throughout the book, and without whose insights and willingness to discuss the mental aspects of tennis there would have been no book.

I am grateful, too, to the representatives who helped to get me together with the players, and I owe particular thanks in this regard to Bud Stanner, Frank Craighill, Mike Cardoza, Jim Hamberchen, Mike Narracott, and Jan Steinmann.

Bill Jarrett, an editor, gave me some much needed direction, especially during the early phases of the project, and Larry Sheehan's editing of the final manuscript proved to be most valuable.

I appreciate the patience of Ken Bowden, Paul Menneg and Marv Brown, who gave me the extra time I needed to do the job I wanted to do. And, as always, I am indebted to my wife, Karen, and my children, Lauren and Andrew, for their patience.

Contents

TENNIS
and the Mind

INTRODUCTION

Tennis:
The Mental Dimension

*You can go out on court some days and feel so
sharp and so alert that the ball comes over the
net looking as big as a soccer ball, and you think
to yourself there's no way I can make a mistake.
Other days you can go out and play as if you're in
a fog, unsure of everything. I can remember a
match I played in Spain once against Borg when
my mind was miles from the court and I had no
real awareness of what I was doing except that
I was getting beaten badly. The next day I played
doubles and everything was back to normal. Can I
explain the difference? I wish I could, but I can't.
I can only say that tennis is a game you can never
take for granted.*

                                           ROD LAVER

NOBODY who plays tennis with any degree of pas-
sion needs reminding that there is to the game
a mental dimension that frequently transcends its
purely physical, technical and intellectual demands.

Every one of us, from touring pro to C-level club player, knows what it's like to feel "on" or "off," to feel "loose" or "tight," to experience streaks in which everything that comes off our racquet goes for a winner, as if directed by some superterrestrial force, and to suffer through nightmarish streaks in which the simplest of shots poses a challenge of Herculean proportions, as if we'd never before held a racquet. We know these feelings and yet few of us can either understand or control them.

Tennis, of course, is hardly the only sport in which factors about which we know very little and over which we seem to exercise sparse control go a long way to determine our level of performance on a day in and day out basis, but tennis does embody, it seems to me, a certain uniqueness. For if it shares with other sports the basic problem of executing certain physical acts requiring a highly precise combination of timing, coordination and stamina, tennis asks us to perform these tasks amid an ever changing panorama of circumstances, and at a frequency rate a good deal more intense than in other sports—as often as once every few seconds. (It is one thing to rub your stomach and pat your head simultaneously and something else again to do it *allegro vivace* while you're trying to memorize the Gettysburg Address.)

What's more, the stop-and-go rhythm of tennis—a far cry from the constant flow of, say, soccer or hockey or basketball—coupled with the necessity of shifting mental gears so often—offensive one moment, defensive the next—imposes on the mind of a tennis player burdens whose proper responses run counter to the manner in which the mind tends to operate most effectively. Tennis presents the mind lots of open time sequences in which the mind can spawn its own distractions. Tennis forces the mind into abrupt switches in neutral transmission that make it more vulnerable to temporary transmission breakdowns—breakdowns that invariably produce technical breakdowns on the court.

Let us add to these sizable challenges the fact that tennis is an individual sport (doubles notwithstanding) in which we have the potential to inflict as much damage on ourselves as on our opponents. Most sports provide avenues for self-destruction but not to the extent that tennis does. You blow a layup or foul shot in basketball, you miss an open goal with a hockey shot, kick an easy grounder, or drop a pass in the end zone— these lapses, agonizing as they are, don't automatically put points on the scoreboard for the other side. In tennis nearly every mistake you make usually results in a point for the other side. Few activities known to man seem more ideally suited to the masochistic temperament.

These are not complaints. To the contrary, the mental challenges unique to tennis account, in my view, for the game's remarkable appeal. They help to explain why tennis has a way of getting under the skin of even the neophyte player and help to explain why the game can be, in the literal sense, psychologically addicting. Forget for the moment the sheer fun of the game—the pleasure of movement, the visceral kick that comes from striking a moving ball with a racquet—few other sports offer as many opportunities within as compressed a time period to meet so many varied challenges. Few other sports offer so many chances so often at performing so brilliantly or so ineptly. "The great appeal of tennis," says a tennis-playing psychiatrist named Leon Tec, "is that you never have to wait very long for another chance. No matter how badly you do on one shot, you can always think to yourself I have another chance, and another. Very few activities in life give us this same opportunity."

But if tennis offers the prospect of perpetual redemption, it also denies us the luxury of complacency. "It's such an elusive game," Rod Laver likes to say. "You never really master it. You're never really sure when you go out to play just how you're going to be hitting the ball. You're never really sure afterward just why you played so well or so badly."

Tennis is indeed an elusive game. One reason, certainly, is that the very physical laws of the game present very little in the way of margin of error. A split second either way, an inch or two difference on the hitting surface, a few degrees difference in the racquet angle—all have an enormous impact on what the ball does. But a bigger reason, I think, is that how well or how poorly we are playing at any stage in a tennis match is largely tied up with that most elusive of entities—the mind: how well (or poorly) we're concentrating; how confiden (or tentative) we feel; how keen (or unkeen) we are to win.

Not that these mental considerations in and of themselves are going to produce good tennis. Hitting a tennis ball is, after all, a motor skill, and a highly developed one at that. Denied this basic skill, the most disciplined mind brimming with self-confidence and white hot with competitive desire isn't going to take you very far in the game. No, we're talking here in relative terms. Technical skill is one thing. Having the mental equipment to utilize this technical skill to its maximum potential is something else. "We all know how to hit the ball," Billie Jean King insists, "But what separates the good player from the great player is something that has nothing to do with technique and everything to do with the mind."

Which brings us to *Tennis and the Mind.* The book is primarily an exploration into the mental facets of the game—particularly into the areas of concentration, nerves, and competitive desire. It is not a "how-to" book—at least not in the strict sense of the term. There are no formulas, no mantras, no five easy steps to a more responsive tennis mind. What the book does is to flesh out and examine facets of tennis that people have been talking about for years and years—without really understanding. We all take for granted that good concentration habits are essential to good tennis, but what do we really *mean* by concentration, and why is it so difficult to attain and control. We all take for granted that it feels differently to serve at match point than at 40–love in the first set, but nowhere in the growing mountain of tennis literature that has been accumulating over the past fifty years has anybody really tried to go beyond the obvious in explaining why. We all know that confidence produces better tennis and a lack of confidence makes you play worse, but not many people have ever tried to explain just what it is that produces fluctuations in confidence.

All of which is another way of saying that, compared to what other tennis books have concentrated on in the past, much of the material covered in *Tennis and the Mind* is fairly virgin territory. The number of tennis books on the market today is in the hundreds. Yet only two books of any real substance, *The Inner Game of Tennis* and *Inner Tennis,* by Tim Gallwey, are addressed to the purely mental side of the game. And neither of these books, as important and as original as they are, really *explores* the mental side of tennis as much as each delineates a certain theory of how best to deal with the mental pressures of the game.

Tennis and the Mind offers no single theory. My chief sources of information for this book were the people who, it seems to me, are in the best position to talk about the mental facets of tennis—the top players on the professional tour. If any one theme emerges from the book, it is that the top players are as individual in the way they deal with the mental pressures of tennis as they are in the way they stroke the ball. What works, mentally, for Bjorn Borg doesn't necessarily work for Ilie Nastase or Rod Laver. What produces "mental toughness" in Billie Jean King doesn't necessarily produce the same results for Chris Evert. Indeed, in the final analysis, what we normally think of as mental toughness turns out to be not so much a single quality but a generalized mental state that arises when a player successfully adapts his or her own personality patterns to meet the mental pressures inherent in specific tennis situations.

You may wonder whether the experience of professional players within the mental sphere of tennis represents a valid model for the recreational player. I think it does, although there is obviously a point at which connections between the professional game and the club game become tenuous at best. I have tried throughout the book to keep in mind the vast differences between the groups, and I can't imagine a club player not being able to draw from the book insights and even some specific techniques that will make a difference in his or her own ability to deal with the mental side of tennis.

A brief word here about my credentials. I have been playing tennis for about eight years and have been writing about it for the past five years. I am neither an expert player nor an expert in mind function. My interest in the mental side of the game is partially the result of my own struggles with tennis and it has been further fueled by an interest in the physiology of mind function that arose several years ago when I collaborated with a Swarthmore College professor on a textbook on physiological psychology. It has been my good fortune, too, over the past five years to have worked closely with a number of top professional players—Rod Laver, Roy Emerson, Dennis Ralston, and Manuel Orantes—on books that, while they did not deal with the mental side of tennis per se, did afford me insights into the workings of a tennis player's mind that I would not have been able to get through simple interviewing techniques.

But these factors notwithstanding, it would be both presumptuous and naïve of me to present *Tennis and the Mind* as the ultimate work on the subject. It is, to repeat a word I used earlier, an exploration into an area of tennis that nobody—not even the players who have seemingly mastered it—completely understands. We're dealing, remember, with an entity—the mind—whose workings are enigmatic even to the scientists most deeply involved in the study of it. Whether the mystery will ever be solved is a question I am certainly not equipped to answer. But one thing seems reasonably certain: as long as the overall mystery of the mind remains unsolved, tennis will retain its tantalizingly elusive quality. And I, for one, would be the last person to wish for a hasty solution.

I

Controlling the Mind

The key to concentration is going out on the court and not allowing anything that might be going on in your private life to interfere with what you have to think about in tennis. I myself have trouble doing this, but it affects me in different ways. Sometimes, when I have a lot on my mind, I actually play better than I normally do. Other times, I play worse. It's something I can never predict.

CHRIS EVERT

DENNIS RALSTON was having a hard day's night—the sort of night that would make a player at any level of the game wonder what ungodly forces lured him into tennis in the first place. Teamed with Arthur Ashe in an early-round doubles match against Billy Martin and Dickie Dell in the 1975 Pacific Southwest Championships, Ralston, a superb doubles player normally, seemed to be doing everything in his power—double faulting, botching overheads, spraying his service returns all over the court—to make sure that Martin and

Dell came away with the victory. On one crucial point, he looked so inept butchering a volley that a man next to me in UCLA's Pauley Pavilion shook his head and muttered, "Dennis Ralston has about as much right on that court as I do."

At is happens, the man was right, but not for the reasons he may have thought. In the midst of a comeback following his ouster as the U.S. Davis Cup captain and coach, Ralston actually had been playing well lately, but in this particular match, his mind was burdened with concerns that had nothing to do with tennis—a situation I was aware of only because he and I were collaborating at the time on a book. Two weeks before there had been a fire at Ralston's newly built Bakersfield, California home, and ever since, Ralston, his wife, and their three children had been living in a house with no working kitchen. If this wasn't disrupting enough, Ralston was simultaneously engaged in some difficult business negotiations with a local resort. And on the very morning of the Martin/Dell match, his six-year-old son had gotten into a scrap with another boy and had been sent home from school, necessitating an early afternoon meeting between Dennis, his wife, and the school principal. By the time everything had been smoothed out, it was close to five o'clock, and Ralston had to make the 120-mile drive to Los Angeles in less than two hours—no easy trick during the rush hour. "I hate to make excuses," Ralston sighed after his match that night, "but it's tough to get mentally ready when you're not even sure you're going to get to the match on time."

I relate this story not to defend a bad night in the career of Dennis Ralston, or even to dramatize a point that sports spectators are not always sensitive to—namely, that professional athletes are subject to many of the same domestic pressures that hassle everybody else. The real point here is that even for a professional tennis player, somebody who has been working at the game nearly every day of his life for more than a quarter of a century, there are occasions when the mind simply refuses to cooperate with the body on the tennis court and will not permit the body to do what it knows how to do. This being the case for professionals, is it any wonder that the inability to keep your mind in line throughout a match—which is to say, to concentrate—is to tennis at all levels what the common cold is to medicine?

A definition of terms, if you please. Concentration can be best described, in tennis terms, as the ability to achieve—*and sustain*—a mental groove in which tennis, and only tennis, occupies center stage in the mind. The consequences that result when concentration fails take any number of forms: you mishit shots; you move sluggishly; you play inconsistently; you hit the wrong shot at the wrong time. The bottom line, however, is the same: your game is "off." As Cliff Richey likes to put it, "Some days you're there on the court but not really there."

On the surface, keeping your mind on tennis throughout a match would seem an easy enough enterprise. A question of habit. Mind over matter. Granted, the mind is bound to drift now and then, but all you have to do when this happens, it would seem, is to draw in a few deep breaths and start focusing on the ball again. O.K., guys, you've had your weekend blast. Now it's time to get back to work.

Not quite. Frequently the mind is curiously unreceptive to simple commands. You order yourself to think about the ball and seconds later you're thinking about what you're going to eat for dinner or what you're going to tell your boss the next time he rides you. You prod yourself to move, but you remain lead-footed. You make up your mind to wear down your opponent's backhand, and you find yourself hitting every ball to his forehand.

To be sure, the arbitrary and mercurial nature of the mind is hardly a phenomenon confined to the tennis court. Actors, singers, writers—even business executives and salesmen—experience days when the mind is fuzzy, balky, when it refuses to stay in one place, when it races and skids like a car out of control on an ice slick. Frequently there is a reason: fatigue, illness, preoccupation with a personal crisis. But what's curious —and fascinating—about the workings of the mind, especially on the tennis court, is that it can take leave even when none of these disruptive agents are in the neighborhood. At Wimbledon one year, for instance, Lew Hoad, the great Australian star of the 1950s, was leading in a match by two sets to one when he suddenly found himself struggling to remember the name of a boxer from Thailand who had recently won the world's bantamweight championship. "The boxer's name was so unusual," recalls Hoad, a boxing fan since his youth, "that I started thinking about it more than I did the match. As a result, I ended up losing."

Hoad's experience at Wimbledon is not extraordinary. Most world-class tennis players will tell you that at times during matches, his or her mind becomes inexplicably preoccupied with images or thoughts that have nothing to do with what is happening on the tennis court. Stan Smith remembers that after he'd taken a two-set lead in the 1971 Wimbledon final against John Newcombe, he began to ponder what song he would

ask the orchestra to play when he and Evonne Goolagong (who'd already won the women's final) danced
the victory dance that night. He's convinced that
musing about the song took the edge from his game and
was one of the factors that enabled Newcombe to win
the next three sets. Arthur Ashe sometimes finds himself thinking about song lyrics at different and unpredictable times in a match. Ralston remembers big
matches in Europe and Australia when his mind would
suddenly cross the ocean, and he'd begin thinking about
his family. Clark Graebner says that even in the middle
of a long rally he would, at times, find himself focusing
not on the ball but on the face of a world figure or enter-
tainer he'd read about earlier in the day.

Club players, in this respect, turn out to be no different from the pros. I once asked a group of players
at an indoor club, what sort of thoughts darted in and
out of their minds during the course of an hour of tennis. A doctor said he once lost a club tournament
match at night because he was haunted throughout by
the feeling that he'd left his car lights on. A high school
tennis player said she ran into a slump while she was
reading Thoreau. ("Every time I'd walk back into position between points, I'd think about the guy up at the
pond.") Several women said that they cannot think
about tennis if any of their children are ill. One woman
boldly admitted to me that her biggest problem in
mixed doubles was, "wondering what the guy serving
to me would be like in bed."

Such mental flights from the *Sturm und Drang* of
tennis combat are obviously not the stuff from which
tennis excellence is forged. And for a good reason.
To properly execute a tennis stroke presupposes a
sequence of incredibly complex and systematized

neurological and physiological events involving billions of circuits throughout the nervous system. The sequence begins as soon as your eyes pick up the ball off your opponent's racquet. The sequence doesn't end until the ball you've hit is on its way to the other side of the court. What takes place in the interim can best be described as inter-cellular communication—a flood of electrical impulses being shuttled back and forth between the eyes, the brain and all the various muscle groups that produce the swing, with the whole shooting match produced, directed and choreographed by the brain. A major production. If, in a future life, you are offered the left arm of Rod Laver, don't take it. Hold out for the brain that tells it what to do.

Exactly how this whole process takes place is anybody's guess, but it's been proven time and again in the laboratory and in clinical cases that if you disrupt the communication circuits in the nervous system you throw a monkey wrench into the behavioral works, and with predictably chaotic results. Injury and disease can disrupt the circuits, but so can other less sinister agents. A fit of anger can do it. So can a momentary seizure of fear. So can an errant thought. In any event, the more complex the activity, the more complex the circuitry that underlies it and, not surprisingly, the more vulnerable is this circuitry to breakdowns.

But complexity is a relative concept. If your name is Jimmy Connors and you're having a friendly little hit between tournaments, you can come to the court with three-fourths of the brain's neural forces out to lunch and still give a pretty fair imitation of a tennis player. Repetition does it. Years of hitting and hitting and hitting establish in the nervous system of a Connors, or of any accomplished player, a remarkably specialized network of neural circuitry. Like an automated camera that does its own focusing and F-stop adjusting, the mind of a professional player requires little more than a simple cue. From then on, everything sort of hums into place. The brain is at the controls but it can relax, like a pilot on a plane equipped with automatic pilot.

Not so with beginning or intermediate tennis players. Oh, there is circuitry being formed, and plenty of signals being relayed back and forth, but the activity is not exactly a model of ease and efficiency. The brain, having an idea of how things should go, pushes the right buttons. But the responses don't come the way they should. Neural signals keep colliding, like bumper cars in an amusement park. The brain thrashes around: the helpless commander of an atomic submarine who has just been asked to go on maneuvers with a shipload of green scrubs. Had my own brain been given the opportunity during the first year or so I played tennis it would have requested a transfer.

All of which brings us to concentration and its role in tennis. In and of itself, it cannot prod the body into manufacturing a down-the-line backhand passing shot —not if the circuitry isn't there. But that's not its function. The function of concentration is to produce an inner environment that best enables the existing circuitry to do what it is wired to do. Part of this function is essentially preventive—keeping the circuits free of intrusive inputs (i.e., inputs that have nothing to do with tennis)—but it would be wrong to characterize concentration as a primarily defensive force. There is a subtle but, as we'll see, crucial difference between keeping your mind *on* tennis and keeping your mind *off* matters that have nothing to do with tennis, even though the result is frequently the same.

But more on that later. What is important to keep in mind before we start getting too specific about concentration is that the relationship between what the mind does and how the body responds does not lend itself to easy dissection. Knowing *what* to do or even how to do it is different from being able to do it. The fact that on occasion you can hit a serve that not even a Connors could get his racquet on does not mean that on those more frequent occasions when your serve is from hunger, the problem is in your head. In the majority of instances, shoddy execution in tennis is the result of a faulty technique not faulty thinking. The circuits, or, as Torben Ulrich likes to call them, "the tapes," are simply not there—at least not to the extent that will produce consistency.

Concentration can help but it can't produce miracles. How much it can help—and hurt—you is an open question, the answer depending on who you are, what sort of game you have and what sort of conditions you're playing under. Concentration can be controlled, but only within certain guidelines. And before we can understand what these guidelines are we ought to first get an understanding of the overall process itself—not so much as it relates to tennis but as a mental phenomenon in its own right.

THE CONCENTRATION PROCESS

WHEN psychologists talk about concentration, they usually use the word "attention." Attention refers to a state of mind in which the brain is reacting in a fairly specific way to a specific stimulus or range of stimuli. This is easier said than done. Our daily environment is a jangled carnival of sounds, sights, smells, and touch sensations, and it's up to the brain to respond selectively to only a minute percentage of these inputs.

What helps the brain react selectively is something called the *reticular formation.* The job of the reticular formation is to act as a sort of screening station between the environment and the brain. Like a good secretary, the reticular formation is toughmindedly selective about the stimuli it allows to reach the upper levels of the brain. Only a stimulus with a good story ever gets an audience with the powers that be in the cerebral board room.

Researchers have been trying for a long time to pinpoint the factors that either promote or detract from the state of attention. It's taking time, but they're learning. It's known, for instance, that if a stimulus is inherently strong enough—a blinding light, an ear-deafening sound, an acrid smell, a sharp pain—it doesn't have to navigate the normal reticular formation red tape; it gets the brain's immediate attention, usually at the expense of everything else.

More often, though, a variety of motivations will determine *which* stimuli the mind will attend to. Certain motivations are directly connected to physiological needs such as food, water and oxygen, and a deficit in any of these areas will obviously occupy a good portion of the mind's attention. (Do not ask a man who hasn't eaten in three days if he is interested in a game of mixed doubles. Do not expect yourself to play as well as you normally play if you're a man playing an attractive woman in a revealing tennis outfit.)

Stimulus and motivational state—these two elements

are at work in every situation involving attention. The stronger the stimulus, the less required in the way of motivation to generate an attentive response. The weaker the stimulus, the *more* required in the way of motivation. Supply and demand. If you've ever wondered why, when you start to get very tired in a match, you have a tendency to make flashy volleys but miss easy sitters at the net, I'll tell you. A ball screaming toward your face is inherently a more pressing stimulus. It thus produces a stronger attention response than, say, a lazy lob. In the case of the former, attention is almost a reflex response—like pulling your hand away from a hot stove. In the case of the latter, the attention energy has to originate entirely from within. Sometimes the energy cupboard is bare. (One of the best pieces of advice I've ever received in tennis came from an astute young teaching pro named Butch Trellue. "The easier the shot," he says, "the *more* you have to force yourself to concentrate. When you're hitting a real soft shot near the net, you should squeeze the racquet as if your life depended on it.")

The constantly changing relationship between stimulus, motivation, and energy level explains why concentration for many players has a tendency to come and go, like the sun on a variably cloudy day. On certain points, when no intrusions or distractions have polluted the motivational environment, concentrating on the ball presents no problems. On other points, with distractions having infiltrated the buffer zone, or with energy levels temporarily low, the attention process is compromised.

If distractions represented an *aberration* of mind function, attending to a tennis ball would not be difficult. But the brain's natural tendency is to remain fluid, its sleeping bag and toothbrush never farther than the corner of the room. No matter how much it is attending to one stimulus, the brain is always potentially receptive to other overtures: it will entertain all reasonable propositions. A good thing, too, because part of our ability to survive hinges on the brain's ability to shift its attention very quickly when the situation demands it— to detect the smell of smoke, for instance, even though you're focusing on a chase scene in a TV movie. Self-preservation is a 24-hour-a-day job.

So we bring to the tennis court a brain that will, if we hardnose it, pay attention to the ball, and yet at the same time remain potentially receptive to stimuli that have nothing to do with tennis. Introduce to the brain a face without a name—as happened to Lew Hoad at Wimbledon—and the brain will send out a neural search party deep into the abysses of the nervous system. Never mind that you're in the tiebreaker of the third set of your club championship. Subject the brain's receptors to an unusual sound from a neighboring court, or an uncomfortable sensation—a blister, for instance—and it will draw attention away from the match and toward the new—and more pressing— stimulus.

Forgetting even the damage that such blatantly obtrusive stimuli can do to one's attention, the mind is capable of creating plenty of its own mischief. Once when I went to play tennis at an indoor club in Manhattan, I noticed that one of the players in the adjacent court was Robert Redford. I like Redford as an actor, but given the choice I'd rather play tennis than see any of his movies. Still, it was one hell of a trick keeping my mind *off* Redford and on my tennis. Initially, the discovery that titilated my mind was that Redford isn't as tall in person as he appears to be in the movies. Then there was the voyeuristic curiosity of wanting to know how well he hit (and, I have to admit, when I saw him double fault, I was pleased: why should a guy have everything going for him?).

Eventually, it got out of hand. It dawned on me that when I told my wife, who adores Redford, that I had played in the court next to him, she would have a million questions. Who was he playing? What was he wearing? So a good portion of the time I spent playing tennis in the court next to Robert Redford was not spent thinking about tennis but about whether I was going to tell my wife about it or not. Need I tell you how poorly I played?

So you see. Once a distraction works its way into your consciousness, the disruptive repercussions can be extreme. Feed it any sort of cue—a brief moment of self-reprobation, for instance—and it will make like the New York Philharmonic, producing a symphony of self-remonstrations. The result may not *always* be an error or a poor shot—and it's possible at times that even though your mind is drifting you feel as if you're hitting the ball a lot better—but in a close match, these mental flights will eventually catch up to you. You will lose focus on key points and frequently play the wrong shot. And when the match is over, you'll wonder how you could have played so well and yet lost.

Bjorn Borg:

Very often in a tennis match, you can point to just one game where for a couple of points you lost concentration and didn't do the right thing, and the difference in the match will be right there.

WHY THE MIND DRIFTS

ANY time the mind drifts, whether on a tennis court or anywhere else, there is a reason. Sometimes the reason is no more complicated than simple fatigue (which is why Billie Jean King advises, "The minute you feel yourself getting a little tired, that's when you have to force yourself to concentrate harder"). Sometimes the distractions are so jarring not even the Maharishi could sustain concentration.

For the most part, though, fatigue and jarring distractions are *not* the chief culprits behind concentration lapses. When the mind shifts its focus, most of the time it's because it simply loses interest in whatever it was paying attention to in the first place. The loss of interest can be temporary, but on a tennis court a temporary lapse is all it takes to lose a couple of points, a key game, and, on occasion, a match.

But why should the mind lose interest, even temporarily, when on a conscious level we *want* to stay focused and, in some instances, desperately *care* about what happens on the court?

Well, it's helpful to bear in mind that the mind, even in the midst of a tennis match, is constantly being besieged by nontennis stimuli—sights, sounds, touch sensations, thoughts, even smells, and it's expecting a great deal of the mind to ask it to ignore everything else save the tennis ball. A tennis ball is not an inherently interesting or pressing stimulus. Staying interested in it for long periods of time is no easy matter.

Certain tennis players are much better than others at sustaining interest in the ball, but exactly why is difficult to say. Possibly it has to do with differences in neurophysiological makeup. Some people may be born with a greater potential for attentiveness than others. More and more specialists in the field of learning disabilities now feel, for instance, that subtle differences in brain function account for the inability of some children to block out disruptive stimuli—stimuli that interfere with, say, the words on the page of a book. So it's not unreasonable to suggest that just as players differ widely in the basic arsenal of athletic equipment they bring to the game—balance, coordination, speed, etc.—it's possible that similar variations exist in their attentive processes as well.

But neurophysiological differences apart, it's safe to say that temperament and personality also go a long way to determine a player's attentive capacities. I'm not certain I completely go along with the idea that the tennis court is a Rorschach test of personality, but it does seem that players who are well organized and mentally orderly *off* the court seem less vulnerable to concentration lapses *on* the court. Concentration problems appear to be most chronic among players with more volatile and mercurial personalities. If you were to spend an evening with Chris Evert, for instance, it wouldn't surprise you at all that she can exercise such remarkable mental discipline on a tennis court. And to spend off-court time with Ilie Nastase is to be amazed not so much that he has trouble concentrating on the court, but that a man with such a seemingly short span of attention should be able to concentrate on the court as *well* as he does.

So there are undoubtedly certain "givens"—genetic makeup, personality—that affect concentration, but there also appears to be an enormous potential for variation. There are days when Chris Evert's mental discipline breaks down and days when Ilie Nastase is a paragon of concentration. These same variations affect club players as well—probably even more so.

There are reasons; and one of the biggest is boredom. Not the kind that puts you to sleep during a lecture on the housekeeping habits of the boll weevil, but the intermittent attacks of boredom that occur when the activity on the court is insufficient to entice the full attention of the mind.

The degree of stimulation needed to generate a sustained level of concentration will obviously vary, but nearly every player, regardless of level, needs to feel a certain element of challenge if he is going to sustain concentration. A common problem among otherwise strong players is an inability to perform well against inferior competition—an inability that probably has its source in the absence of a real challenge in these matches. The problem is much less severe in the professional ranks than in the club ranks, where the competition is rarely all that weak and where the rewards that come with victory (prize money, ranking, etc.) represent a challenge unto themselves. But it exists all the same.

Butch Buchholz:

There's one thing you can say about a true champion—a guy that wins big tournaments year after year—and it's that he never gets bored. Take a guy like Lew Hoad. He had more natural talent than anybody I've ever seen, I always felt that it didn't matter to him, really, if he won or not. It was almost as if that knowing he was better than the next guy was all that mattered. Some people said he didn't have good groundstrokes, but he had great groundstrokes. He just found it difficult to stay mentally alert. That was never Laver's problem. Or Gonzales's. Or Segura's. And it's just as true today. Take a player like Panatta: all the ability in the world, but he gets bored. If he had Connors's temperament, he'd never lose.

Rod Laver:

Staying interested in a match is a lot harder than many people think. Throughout my career, I've always had trouble in the early rounds of a tournament mainly because it was hard for me to psychologically get "up" until I got to the quarters or the semis. What happened a lot of times is that I would fall behind early, maybe even lose the first couple of sets in a five-set match and then *begin to concentrate. Still, it wasn't something I could control from the start.*

The pattern described by Buchholz and Laver is not unfamiliar, but it seems to be more prevalent among the very gifted players. Ilie Nastase, for instance, maintains that even if he could win with the style, he would never choose to play tennis in the retrieving baseline style epitomized by players like Harold Solomon, Guillermo Vilas and Eddie Dibbs. "I lose my mind I play like that," he says. "It's not tennis." Bobby Riggs, on the other hand, insists that he could never get interested in a match until he was behind.

Riggs:

I needed the challenge to keep me interested. If the challenge wasn't there, if I was winning easily without any sweat, I'd have difficulty concentrating. The time I was able to concentrate the most was when it got to be 4–4 or something like that in the final set.

We have to be careful about the word "challenge," a highly subjective concept. The amount of challenge needed to light a fire under Bobby Riggs may well be three times the amount needed to motivate Bjorn Borg or Harold Solomon. What's more, the relationship of challenge to attention is not fixed. Few players are more mentally in focus on the court than Bjorn Borg, but even Borg runs into his problems from time to time.

Borg:

Mostly, it happens when I've been playing too much. I might feel all right physically, but mentally I'm tired. I can't really describe the sensation, but what happens is that concentration doesn't come naturally. I have to force myself to do it. And because I'm forcing I often become impatient and angry with myself. The only thing that works for me when I get like this is to lay off for a few weeks. Then when my mind is fresh and I feel keen to play, my concentration comes naturally.

Psychologists call it the "satiation effect." Ring a buzzer in the cage of an experimental rat for the first time and the rat will leap out of its skin. It will *pay attention!* Do it enough times and the rat won't blink an eye at the sound. A similar phenomenon seems to occur on the tennis court with some players. After a certain number of balls, a threshold of sorts seems to be reached. The mind decides it has had enough and seeks diversion elsewhere. Sometimes it tunes out altogether. You go through all the motions, but there's a dimension of awareness missing. Manuel Orantes once described what it's like to play a match in this state of mind.

Orantes:

It happened to me in my fourth-round match against François Jauffret in the 1975 U.S. Open. Usually I don't have much trouble with Jauffret because I know his game and I know how to play him. But for some reason, on this day, I was hitting my shots to his strength—his forehand. I would hit a shot and wonder after I hit why I'd hit there, and then, a minute later, I'd do the same thing. If it wasn't that Jauffret made a lot of errors that day, I would have lost the match.

That night, following the match, Orantes talked it over with his doubles partner, Juan Gisbert, and with Juan's wife, Margaret, whose sister was once a tournament player in Germany:

Margaret felt that I'd been spending too much time on the tennis court—both practicing and playing. She suggested that I not even go to Forest Hills the next day to practice. I took her advice. I canceled my practice court for the next day and my wife and I spent the day touring New York.

*I didn't think about tennis once. The next day,
when I played Ilie Nastase in the quarter-finals,
I played my best match of the tournament.*

The phenomenon we're talking about is, for the most
part, involuntary. It isn't, after all, as if the mind issues
any warnings (although if you find yourself becoming
more irritated than usual, chances are you're being told
something) to the effect that it has had its fill of tennis.
It simply ups and leaves, with not even a note of
thanks. There are some steps, as we shall see, which
can be taken to prevent this from happening, but no
way to really control it. Listen to John Newcombe, who,
in the late 1960s, lost a semi-final match to Tony Roche
when he double faulted twice in a row in the twelfth
game of the fifth set.

Newcombe:

*That match was a good example of some part of
me that I wasn't really in touch with deciding that
it had just had enough. It was a very hot day and
Tony and I had been battling each other for hours.
The match couldn't have been closer and, in the
end, it came down to the fact that deep down Tony
was more strongly motivated to win than I was.
Mentally, he stayed strong, but I had that one
lapse.*

One lapse. That's all it takes sometimes to lose a
match. Exactly why certain players should be more
prone to such lapses is not really known, but many of
the professional players feel that it comes down to
what Newcombe described as "wanting it bad

enough." Clark Graebner, a world-class player in the late 1960s, elaborates.

Graebner:

What used to happen to me in some matches and against some players, is that I'd find it difficult sometimes to stay interested in a point if it went on for too long—or even in a match if it was just kind of bumping along. At the time, I'd get angry with myself if I lost, but now that I look back on it, I have a feeling that the real problem was that I didn't really want it that bad. I didn't have this burning ambition to be the greatest tennis player in the world, and at certain times, in certain matches, the lack of this desire is what cost me my concentration.

Let us be careful. It's possible to interpret from Graebner's remarks a rationalization for losing, the implication being that a player whose concentration deserts him in a crunch may be actually choking in a way that he finds psychologically palatable. But by and large, the pattern described by Graebner appears to apply mostly to the professional players whose off-court lives are the most diverse and stimulating. Remember we're talking here about *subconscious* factors—factors that may never surface in a match. Still, if a struggle between two comparable players is intense and is taking place under severe enough conditions—a brutally hot day, for instance—it is a safe assumption that the player who has the stronger motivation is going to sustain concentration better than the player whose mind is not fully committed to this sort of struggle.

Cliff Richey:

*I'm not sure I understand exactly why it happens
—maybe it's a physical thing—but I'm convinced
that every player has a breaking point—a point
when the pressure gets to be so much that his
mental attitude starts to work against him instead
of for him, and, no matter what he does, his concentration starts to go. One of the things I always
had going for me when I was playing my best was
the feeling I had that it was going to happen to the
other player first.*

KEEPING THE MIND IN TOW

THE fact that lapses in concentration generally
occur involuntarily, fueled by subconscious factors
over which we have no real control, doesn't necessarily
mean that such lapses are unavoidable. Far from it.
Indeed, it's the ability to stay mentally keen throughout a match that frequently differentiates the top
players from the second level players. But how do they
do it and, more to the point, what do the pros do that
can help the concentration powers of the average
player?

There are no easy answers. The pros, to begin with,
enjoy one enormous advantage over the average club
player. Tennis is the chief and, sometimes, *only* focal
point in their lives. I once asked Neale Fraser, the
former Wimbledon and Forest Hills champ and coach
of Australia's Davis Cup team, just what it was about
Australian players that made them, as a group, so much

more immune to the distractions that spoil the concentration of other players. His reply was so obvious, I
felt silly that I'd asked the question.

Fraser:

*Look at it this way. If, from the age of ten, you
had done almost nothing else in your life but hit
tennis balls, and had thought about and talked
about almost nothing but tennis, you'd probably
find it easy to think about tennis and nothing but
tennis on the court, too. The reason a lot of players
concentrate so well on the court is that they really
don't have anything else to think about.*

Not a particularly reassuring answer, I grant you, but
don't dismay. There are a number of players who, while
they agree with Fraser's basic premise, still feel that
concentration is something that anybody, regardless of
how often he plays, can improve.

Laver:

*There's no secret to building concentration. It's
something you develop the same way you develop
other parts of your game. The mistake most club
players make is that they don't practice concentration while they're practicing their strokes. If
your mind is going to wander during practice, it's
going to do the same thing in a match. When we
were all growing up in Australia, we had to work
as hard mentally as we did physically in practice.
If you weren't alert, you could get a ball hit off the
side of your head. What I used to do was to force
myself to concentrate more as soon as I'd feel myself getting tired, because that's usually when your*

concentration starts to fail you. If I'd find myself getting really tired in practice, I'd force myself to work much harder for an extra ten or fifteen minutes, and I always felt as though I got more out of those extra minutes than I did out of the entire practice.

Laver's feeling that concentration can be practiced is shared by most of the top players, chief among them Billie Jean King, whose workouts are described here by her frequent practice partner, Vicki Berner.

Berner:

Billie would pick one shot—a crosscourt backhand, for instance—and we'd keep hitting them until we'd hit forty good ones in a row. Then we'd take another stroke and do the same thing and keep trying for forty good shots in a row for every shot. What's good about a drill like this is that it gets you accustomed to keeping your concentration during long rallies. And if you can keep up your concentration in long practice rallies, you're much better prepared for them in a match.

Chris Evert seems to have developed her remarkable powers of concentration in much the same way, working not just on technique and accuracy but on consistency.

Evert:

Basically, what my dad and I used to do in my practice sessions was to keep hitting as many balls as we could without a miss. With me, concentration developed so naturally that I rarely have to force myself to do it. It's part of my game.

Dennis Ralston has gone so far as to formulate a special sequence of drills that he recommends to all the players he coaches.

Ralston:

It's based on something an old coach of mine told me—that once I could hit a particular shot twenty times in a row, I could consider that shot mastered. I tell the players I coach to set up a sequence for themselves: forehand drive; backhand drive; forehand volley; backhand volley; serve. The idea is to hit twenty in a row of each shot without a miss. If you miss one shot, you have to go all the way back to the beginning. A drill like this forces you to concentrate, even when you start getting a little tired or a little bored. The reason a lot of the pros can't beat players like Borg or Vilas or Solomon is that they've never developed the concentration needed to keep the ball in play that long.

A few players go to unconventional lengths to enhance concentration. Two of them are Torben Ulrich, the bearded Dane who is presently the world's No. 1 over-forty-five player, and Jeff Borowiak, the tall, black-haired Californian, whose concepts of mind control in tennis have have been shaped in large part by Ulrich. I will not attempt at this point to explain in depth what these concepts are, except to say that Ulrich cannot be understood in the same way you can understand, say, Dennis Ralston or Billie Jean King. His is the path of the Bhagavad-Gita, not Vince Lombardi. Borowiak's description of how he and Torben practice together, when they happen to be in Copenhagen at the same time, will show you what I mean.

Borowiak:

We go to the indoor center very late at night, when no one else is there. That's when Torben likes to practice best. We begin by just sitting quietly and staring at the ball for about ten minutes. Then we complicate it by jumping up and down, counting our breaths up to fifty, but always watching the ball. Then we might run back and forth from one side of the court to the other—still looking at the ball. Another exercise we do is to crawl on all fours, pushing the ball ahead of us with our hands, always keeping the ball in view.

Bizarre as these drills may seem to somebody not schooled in the ways of Zen, they are not without their psycho-physiological logic. The idea here is to train the mind to stay engrossed with the ball for long periods of time, amid the distraction of increasingly more complicated physical activity. Borowiak maintains that after he does these drills, it is much easier for him to sustain concentration in a match. "I can *see* the ball better," he says, using "see" in a manner that goes beyond "watching" the ball, reflecting the attention process in the positive extreme.

But despite these special drills, not even Borowiak is immune to concentration lapses. One such distraction probably cost him a victory in a semi-final match against Guillermo Vilas in the 1975 Firemen's Fund Open in San Francisco. Borowiak had just lost his serve in the final set, putting Vilas ahead 5–4. He'd been playing well up to that point, but suddenly in the last game his strokes fell apart, and he lost on four straight unforced errors.

Borowiak:

I don't know exactly what happened. I know that I was disappointed about losing my serve in the ninth game. And I started to think about how I had lost the serve—whether I hadn't served hard enough or what—instead of thinking about the next game and trying to break back Guillermo. I had an image of myself as a race car driver who was leading in a race the whole time and suddenly lost the lead. It was a distraction, and I just wasn't ready to play that last game. I wasn't ready to deal with it.

PREVENTING DISTRACTIONS

HAVING a network of mental machinery with the capacity for sustaining concentration over long periods of time is one thing. Being able to use this machinery to maximum benefit is something else. The top players recognize how fragile concentration can be and go to great lengths to prevent breakdowns from occurring.

It begins with what can best be described as "mental preparation." We know far less about what it takes to prepare *mentally* for a match than we do about how to get physically prepared, but basically mental preparation involves keeping the mind as free as possible from any inputs that may sabotage the concentration process. Ideally, the preparation process should begin long before the match you're scheduled to play is due to take place. Witness the remarkable success the Mexican star Raul Ramirez was able to enjoy in 1974 and 1975 against the U.S. Davis Cup team. Three weeks before Ramirez singlehandedly beat the U.S. team in Mexico City, in December 1975, Ramirez did so poorly in the Grand Prix Masters, I couldn't see how he stood a chance against the American stars. The following January, two weeks after his victory, Ramirez had an explanation for the incredible difference between the way he'd played in Mexico City against Jimmy Connors and Brian Gottfried, and the way he played in Stockholm.

Ramirez:

It's definitely the way I prepared myself—mentally and physically. When I'm getting ready for Davis Cup, I don't have to think about anything except my tennis. Everything else is taken care of for me. All the little details of life—arranging for meals, laundry, making practice arrangements— it's all taken care of. I have nothing else to think about except getting ready. I have no other distractions.

I've pondered Ramirez's explanation many times. What he did was to allow himself plenty of time to let potential distractions disappear. I've wondered how my own tennis would be affected if for one entire week prior to a match—especially one that I wanted to win badly—I didn't have to think about my family, my work, my house, the world situation, or anything else that didn't have a direct bearing on my tennis. It would take some doing. Meal schedules, car pools, editor's deadlines—all would have to be rearranged lest they pose a potential distraction. It's a fantasy, I know, but just once it would be nice to hear my wife say to one of my children: "Don't bother your father now, he has an important match next week."

So much for fantasies. Most of us do not enjoy the luxury of a two-week preparation period. If we're going to prepare well, we have to work on a somewhat tighter schedule, like an hour. The principle, however, remains the same: insulate the mind as much as possible.

Jack Kramer:

My feeling about concentration was always this: that I wanted to do as much as I could ahead of time to prevent distractions. I was a creature of routine. It was always important for my peace of mind before a match to have gotten a good night's sleep the night before, to have eaten at the right time—early enough that I wouldn't be bloated, but not so early that I'd be in trouble if I had to play a four-hour match. I was very finicky about my equipment. I always had to make sure that my racquets were strung right, and that I'd gone out and warmed up enough to get a feel for the sun, the wind and the bounce. Other players were different—although even seemingly casual players, like Bobby Riggs, had their own patterns. I found that if I didn't make sure of all these things ahead

*of time, I'd start to think about them a little bit
during the match, and it affected my concentration.*

Most top players tend to be similarly ritualistic. I
was in Las Vegas when Jimmy Connors played Rod
Laver in the first "Heavyweight Championship of Tennis" Challenge Match. Connors arrived at the indoor
pavilion at Caesar's Palace wearing a khaki raincoat
over his tennis clothing. A year later, when Connors
met Manuel Orantes in the third Challenge Match, he
arrived at the indoor pavilion wearing the same raincoat. Connors tends to shrug off questions about these
personal little quirks of his, but, like Kramer, he's obviously a creature of habit. I'm not sure if he still does
it, but Connors once had a habit of always stepping into
the corner of the court each time he walked by a court
in which another pro was practicing.

When and what they eat, when and where they practice, how far in advance of a match they prefer to get
dressed, how many racquets they take with them to the
court, even when they go to the bathroom prior to a
match—each of these considerations, in its own way,
has been programmed by most playing professionals
into an established prematch routine. There is a definite neurophysiological logic to this kind of routine.
The most experienced players appear to know, instinc-
tively, that if you leave open the possibility for a distraction, a distraction will occur. "That's why it's hard
to play tennis when you have any kind of injury," says
Manuel Orantes. "Even when it's *not* hurting, you tend
to wonder when it's going to start."

In moderation, efforts to prevent distractions from
materializing can be viewed as prudent examples of

foresight. But there comes a point at which such efforts leave the realm of foresight and enter the realm of superstition. It's difficult to draw the line between intelligent pre-planning and superstition, but it's probably safe to say that athletes, as a group, are more superstitious than the public at large. Tennis players are no exception.

Some illustrations. Harold Solomon takes a salt pill three hours before he plays every match even though it has been pointed out to him on many occasions that the pill doesn't get into his system until long after three hours. Many players—Tony Roche, for one—are reluctant to make any changes in tennis wardrobe when they're in a hot streak. Arthur Ashe is one of a number of players who tries to dress in the same order every day. Vijay Amitraj tries to get out of bed on the same side on the morning following a match victory. And certain players have hang-ups regarding certain colors. Sashi Menon, the Indian player who doesn't like to wear blue, once explained his phobia to writer Peter Bodo.

Menon:

I'm psyched out if I wear blue. Somehow I'm not loose. I lose if I wear blue. That's a superstition, I suppose, but if I don't wear blue, then I don't have to worry about it. It isn't good to have things bugging you in tennis. You have to take care of that, and have things as smooth and as untroubled as you can. You take care of it any way you can, so you can concentrate on playing.

Superstition apart, most players in the pro ranks show individualistic behavioral patterns in the moments just prior to a match. Some players choose solitude. Others seek out the company of friends, and still others (the minority) show no set pattern at all. In each instance, the purpose seems to be the same: to settle the mind—to keep potential distractions away from fouling up the inner environment.

Ron Holmberg:

I'm pretty sure I went a lot further than most players in getting myself mentally prepared. I used to actually sit down before a match and picture in my mind every possible shot sequence I could imagine that might take place in the match. I'd imagine a short ball coming to my forehand, and I'd picture myself actually making the approach shot and then putting away the volley. I'd imagine myself hitting a drop shot and picture myself moving up to the net to hit a drop shot my opponent hit. In this way, I was able to get my mind into the match even before I stepped onto the court.

Cybernetics, they call it. Mental rehearsal. The theory is that images of certain physical acts can replicate, to some extent, the same physiological processes that take place during the act itself and thus can facilitate learning and improve performance. Not everyone is able to do what Holmberg was able to do. And even players who are able to "rehearse mentally" find the net result unfavorable. Manuel Orantes, for instance, finds that the *worst* thing he can do before a match is to *think* about it. He prefers to sit with his wife or friends and make small talk. If the conversation turns to tennis, he gets up and walks away. Clark Graebner once followed Holmberg's model and with disastrous results.

Graebner:

I sat down and not only thought about each point, I actually chartered it on a piece of paper. It didn't work. I played the worst match of my career.

Professional players also differ widely in the degree of sociability they manifest during pre-match moments. Once, before he was to play Jimmy Connors in a match at North Conway, New Hampshire, Eddie Dibbs was approached by a young autograph-seeker. "I'm not Eddie Dibbs," Dibbs mumbled. "He's on the court."

Dibbs, however, is an extrovert compared to Nancy Gunter. One woman player gave the following account of what Nancy used to be like on the day of battle:

Nancy had a thing about talking to anybody before a match, particularly the girl she was playing. Once when we were scheduled to play later in the afternoon, she came into the locker room at Forest Hills when I was the only one there. She didn't say hello, even though we're friendly. She went over to the locker room girl and asked if there was anybody around she could practice with. I volunteered. We walked out on the court together and still Nancy didn't say a word. I asked if there was anything she wanted to work on and she mumbled a couple of things and that was it. We hit for about an hour, and she never even said thank you when we were finished. She just walked away. The thing about Nancy, though, is that you can't get mad at her. Once a match is over, she's one of the genuinely nicest and most generous women on the tour.

A few of the better known pros give the outward appearance of being remarkably casual before a match, although part of it is undoubtedly an effort to unnerve the opponent. John Newcombe is often boisterous beforehand as though he were already celebrating the victory, but his Australian buddies will tell you that he's giving the match more thought than you might think. Arthur Ashe is another player who seems superficially casual. I once came across Ashe, about fifteen minutes before he was to play an Aetna World Cup match in Hartford, reading Erica Jong's *Fear of Flying*.

Then there's Chris Evert, about whom Julie Anthony says:

It's amazing how casual she can be before a match. Once when we were playing the Wightman Cup, we went out to warm up together on a morning she was scheduled to play. Most girls have a set pattern they go through—a certain number of forehands or backhands, that sort of thing. I asked Chris what she wanted to work on. She shrugged her shoulders and said, "I don't know. What would you like to work on?"

If there is a lesson here, it is that no matter what you do in the hour or so that precedes a match, the idea is to ease into a focused mental groove free of distractions. I have done some experimenting on my own and have found that, even though I may not be consciously aware of any difference in how I feel physically or mentally, I don't play well at all on days when I work at the typewriter up to the last minute before playing. The reason, I'm convinced, is that I haven't given my mind time enough to shift into the right psychological groove. The distractions haven't left the mental arena yet. I'm trying to move one family into a house from which the previous family hasn't left.

Wtih this same situation in mind, Dennis Ralston once gave me the following advice.

Ralston:

You should always give yourself at least ten or fifteen minutes before you play to go through a series of stretching exercises. This will do two things for you: one, it will make you looser and thus help you move better and improve your timing. Two, it will calm your mind and help clear it of the things you were thinking about just before you went out on the court.

You can do even more. Stan Smith, for example, has developed a warm-up routine designed specifically to ease his mind into an attentive state.

Smith:

Some players will start to hit the ball hard right away in the warm-up, or else start thinking about how they're going to play the match. I don't. The only thing I'm concerned about when I warm up is, first, whether or not I'm making contact with the ball in the middle of the racquet. I try to watch the ball actually come off the strings and I don't care if it goes out or into the net. I just want to get the feel of making solid contact. Once I've got that down I start to concentrate on other things, like balance and follow-through. Then, when I really feel comfortable in the stroke, I start worrying about hitting the ball to specific places.

STAYING MENTALLY IN THE MATCH

TRAINING yourself in practice to sustain concentration over long periods of time, and doing your best prior to a match to reach the right mental groove, are basic to the ability to keep the mind on your side throughout a match. The ultimate challenge, though, is to control the mind throughout the ebb and flow of a match.

Roy Emerson:

It starts the minute you walk out on the court. When I'd go out for an important match, I'd look straight down at the ground, as if I were looking for a dime on the court. I never looked at the ball-boys, or the umpire, or even my opponent. I never even listened to anything. All I heard was noise.

Emerson's conscious effort to block out all potentially disruptive stimuli is characteristic of all good players. It is particularly characteristic of Jimmy Connors, who does as effective a job of insulating himself mentally as any player I've ever watched. Connors is all but impervious to distractions and, remarkably, can slip into this groove and still be able to talk and joke with people just prior to a match—"But I won't remember who I talked to or what I said."

On occasion, he'll go even farther. During the first annual Pepsi-Cola Grand Slam of Tennis at Myrtle Beach, South Carolina, Connors played Arthur Ashe on a torridly hot and humid afternoon. Midway through the match, during the changeover, Jimmy began draping a towel over his head.

Connors:

It was hot out there—really hot—but I knew that if I started thinking too much about the sun, I wouldn't do my best. I didn't worry about it while I was on the court, but when I was sitting down, with the sun beating down, it started to get to me a little. So I just blocked it out, and pretended it wasn't there. That's what you have to do in tennis —not let yourself think about anything that can have a negative effect on your game.

The ability to *block out distractions* usually gives one player the mental edge over the other, but distractions can come in any number of guises: a bad call; a string of lucky shots by your opponent; the suspicion that you're getting tired; noise in surrounding courts; thirst; hunger; a blister; crowd reaction. The better players can block them out—but not all of the time.

John Alexander:

I can't tell you exactly how I do it when I'm concentrating well, except that I refuse to allow myself to get involved with anything that doesn't have to do with the match. That's the trap everyone runs into when they play Nastase. He starts to clown around or complain, and pretty soon you're paying more attention to him than you are to your own game.

But there are some players, even in the pros, for whom blocking out distraction throughout the course of a match is a virtual impossibility. Evonne Goolagong is probably one of them.

Julie Anthony:

There's a big difference between concentrating and thinking too much on the court. After a long time, I've finally come to the conclusion the simpler you keep your thinking processes on the court, the better off you are. The best players, by and large, play by instinct—without thinking about them. They are not prone to intellectualizing or trying to logic out a tennis match. Evonne Goolagong is interesting because she's naïve about certain aspects of her game—her tendency to lose concentration, to have what the media has started to call her walkabouts. Well, my feeling is that this tendency of hers to tune out helps her more than it hurts her because it keeps her loose and instinctive.

Evonne is not alone. Lesley Hunt, for instance, is an attractive, likable Australian whose mediocre tournament record is a misleading gauge of her tennis skills. Hunt's problem throughout her career has always been that she does not do well against the weaker players on the tour. Her problem, by her own explanation, is concentration.

Hunt:

I realized I had a problem and so I went to Pancho Segura to see if he could help me. He saw right away where I was going wrong. Against a weaker player, I would get bored and distracted and try to make a lot of flashy shots I had no business trying. That was the only way I could concentrate—except that I wasn't making the shots. What Segura taught me to do was to play different points in a different way—to go for the creative shot when I was ahead, but to play it safer when the score was close. That's one way to stay interested in a match without giving it away.

The therapy worked, but only up to a point. It's questionable whether a player with Hunt's kind of mercurial personality will ever develop the mental discipline needed to play championship caliber tennis consistently. Then again, a lot of people said the same thing about Arthur Ashe prior to his great year in 1975. He was the sort of player, people said, who had too many other things on his mind apart from tennis. Consequently, the big tournament wins would always elude him. So people said.

Ashe once talked about the difference in the mental side of his game throughout 1975.

Ashe:

I honestly can't say that my mind was any less distracted in 1975 than it had been before. I'm always going to have distractions, because tennis itself is not enough to fulfill my life. The things that made a difference were, first, that I trained a lot harder and was not getting so tired in my matches. And, second, I learned to deal with the distractions better. Instead of fighting them all the time, I would let a thought come and go naturally.

Living with the distraction instead of fighting it. This is Ashe's way of staying mentally in tune with what he's doing on the court. There are many variations on the theme. When Rod Laver gets the feeling that he's not being attentive enough, he focuses on his feet.

Laver:

If I can get my feet moving, then everything falls into place a little better for me. Usually, when a player isn't concentrating well, it will show up in one or two technical areas, like not watching the ball, or not getting the shoulders turned. So rather than simply telling yourself to concentrate, the thing you want to do is focus on that one thing that's giving you trouble.

This advice says more than you might think. Embodied in it is a set of directions that the mind can deal with—"specificity," as a New York teaching professional named Warren McGoldrick would call it:

Any time you can key on something concrete to focus on, you're going to get better results than if you give it some very general instruction, like "concentrate." I teach a simple method. You breathe in when the ball strikes your opponent's racquet. You breathe out when you hit. Focusing on the breathing forces you to focus on the ball.

Funny thing. If you talk to most professional players about what they do when they feel their concentration slipping a little, this is exactly what they do: they *specify.* They key on something tangible. Pancho Segura tells his students to pay close attention to the score, to play each point differently. Roy Emerson has trained himself to wipe from memory the preceding point and to focus only on the *next* point. Chris Evert, in those rare moments when her concentration lags, follows the ball as if it were attached to her retina. Roscoe Tanner watches the other player closely. Dennis Ralston counts off the number of points he needs to win in order to take the game. Connors, when he played Orantes in Las Vegas, decided ahead of time that he wasn't going to miss too many of Manuel's low spinning shots the way he did at Forest Hills, and so he went into the match determined, in his words, to "crawl to the ball." Billy Talbert says he used to think about firming the wrist when he felt himself getting mentally sloppy. And Marty Riessen goes so far as to write himself little notes—simply to remind himself to concentrate on certain things, like lobbing.

Forgive me for racing through these examples, but I have a reason. In almost every instance while I was gathering this information, I thought to myself, "Hey, that could work for me." And it did. Tailoring my strategy according to the score, as Segura suggested, did keep my mind on the point; and telling myself, as Connors did in Las Vegas, to "crawl" to low shots did eliminate errors on those shots. Thinking about the wrist, as Talbert suggested, did help me regain a nice groove. The only problem was that while I was concentrating on one part of my game, some other part would develop a kink. My low shots would be working, but I would be double faulting. I would be playing my points intelligently but missing shots; and when I wasn't missing shots (because I was keying on my wrist), I wasn't playing intelligently.

I can't be too harsh on my mind. It is cooperating, up to a point. It will focus on the serve when I order it to do so, and it will take note of my opponent's weak-nesses and even formulate a strategy of sorts. It wants to help, and it's not, I don't think, unduly influenced by subconscious motivations. The problem is much more basic. Put my mind in Jimmy Connors's body and his mind in my body, and my mind would whip his love and love. It isn't that Jimmy Connors expends more mental energy than I do in a tennis match; it's that he can afford the luxury of *specificity* far more than I can. Our mental armies may be similar in size, but his is oc-cupying an orderly land with a docile population. Mine is confronted with guerrilla fighters behind every bush.

CONCENTRATION: THE INNER GAME APPROACH

TIM Gallwey's directions were short and to the point. "I don't want you to consciously think about concentration or watching the ball. All I want you to do is say 'bounce' when the ball hits the ground and 'hit' when the ball hits your racquet. That's all: 'bounce, hit.' "

We were in the driveway of Tim Gallwey's home in Encino, California, and I was taking a lesson of sorts against a small backboard about the size of a Little League scoreboard. Gallwey, the author of the two biggest-selling tennis books in history—*The Inner Game of Tennis* and *Inner Tennis*—has his own views on concentration, and they are not at all conven-tional.

Another pause for definitions.

"Inner Game" is the name Tim Gallwey created to de-scribe the process of dealing with those obstacles to better tennis that originate *within* the tennis player—as opposed to *external* obstacles, such as the net and opposing players. The biggest inner obstacle, in Gallwey's view, is that part of our psyche that he refers to as Self 1. Self 1 is the ego-mind: the conscious, judgmental side of our behavioral apparatus that does all the thinking and worrying, makes all the decisions and judgments. Self 1 is the voice that tells us that we have a big second serve coming up, that we'd better toss the ball higher and swing easier. Self 1 is also the voice that tells us how incredibly stupid we are when we toss the ball higher and swing easier and the ball fails to clear the net. Self 1 is obviously a good voice to have around in many facets of our lives; but on the tennis court, according to Gallwey, it just gets in our road. It doesn't enhance concentration, it disrupts it.

> *The least efficient way to do anything with your body is to consciously try to do it. In tennis, the minute you let yourself become too consciously involved with* why *it's important for you to hit a stroke a particular way, or* why *it's important for you to make a point, you are setting up an obstacle between what you're trying to do and what you have to do in order to hit the shot the way you want to.*

Self 2, on the other hand, is that part of our behavioral apparatus that already *knows* what to do on the tennis court and would be able to execute the proper shots without difficulty were it not for the meddlesome Self 1. What Self 2 doesn't already know, it can absorb very easily—so long as Self 1 doesn't get too involved.

The basic message of Inner Game tennis can be

summed up in three words: "Let it happen." *Allow* the body to do what it wants to do; don't try to *will* the mind to do what you want it to do. Instead, create an inner environment in which the mind will naturally do what it must do.

But how does one create such an environment? Gallwey doesn't oversimplify. He concedes that distractions are lurking everywhere, adding that "even yogis who practice concentration on a single object such as a rose or a flame rarely succeed in stilling the mind for long; it simply loses interest and then wanders." His prescription, from *The Inner Game of Tennis:*

> *As silly as it may sound, one of the most practical ways to increase concentration on the ball is to learn to love it. Get to know the tennis ball; appreciate its qualities. Look at it closely and notice the fine patterns made by the nap. Forget for a moment that it is a tennis ball and look freshly at its shape, its texture, its feel. Consider the inside of the ball and the role played by the empty middle. Allow yourself to know the ball both intellectually and through your senses. Make friends; do anything to start a relationship with it. It will help concentration immeasurably.*

Interpret this slice of Gallwey's book too literally, and it's easy to see why some people find him difficult to take seriously. Sure, Billie Jean King stares at a tennis ball, too. But there is, after all, a qualitative difference between a staring contest and a full-blown relationship. (Who's to say that the ball will be receptive to your overtures? Might not an English ball have a prejudice against an American player?)

Still, when Gallwey talks of the need to develop more

than a casual relationship with the ball in order to improve concentration, he is on solid neurophysiological footing. For as we become more involved with the tennis ball, so do priorities that underlie the workings of the reticular formation change in response to this involvement. And the result, theoretically, is that we concentrate without having to think about it.

When it works, it's beautiful.

Manuel Orantes, on his 1975 Forest Hills victory over Jimmy Connors:

I can't remember ever playing a match in which I was so focused on what I was doing and yet so unconscious about it. I was making all the right decisions, but not consciously thinking about them.

The pros call it "the zone." Everything is working for you without any conscious thought. You're playing on what Gene Scott likes to call "automatic pilot."

That it's possible to pay attention on a tennis court without making a conscious effort to do so has some intriguing implications, assuming it really happens this way. Some researchers in the rapidly growing field of biofeedback, have begun to theorize that there is indeed a mental state that might be best described as "super attention," and that a person in this state would generate a specific, albeit unusual, brain-wave pattern. Inasmuch as the present state of biofeedback hardware precludes the monitoring of an athlete's brain-wave pattern while he is actually competing, it is impossible to say for certain if there is indeed a state of so-called super attention. But in the event there is something to this theory, it then follows that an athlete could be trained, using present biofeedback training tech-

niques, to artificially create this state and thus circumvent the normal obstacles to attention. Like I said, it's
only a theory.

It's also fun to tinker around with some of the ideas
relating to concentration in sports that have been gen-
erated by the transcendental meditation movement.
Some advocates maintain that people who practice TM
regularly find that their concentration powers increase
quite dramatically. The fact that a number of top tennis
players—Arthur Ashe, Roscoe Tanner, Bob Lutz—have
joined a number of noted athletes in other sports in taking up TM has tended to reinforce the notion.

I've talked about TM to Ashe, Tanner, and Lutz, and
their observations do not lend credence to the notion
that practicing TM is measureably going to help your
concentration on the tennis court. A lot of people have
credited Ashe's victory at Wimbledon to the meditating
he was supposed to be doing in between games, but
Ashe points out that he didn't start with TM until *after*
Wimbledon.

Ashe:

*I can't say one way or the other what TM has done
for my tennis. It helps me sleep at night and helps
me to relax, but I'd never meditate before a match
because I simply wouldn't feel like competing.*

Tanner:

*I really didn't notice any difference in my ability
to concentrate after I started meditating. The
thing I got from TM was the ability to overcome
the fact that I'd only got a few hours' sleep the
night before, but I can't see any direct benefits to
my tennis.*

I liked Bob Lutz's analysis the best. "I'm not winning any more frequently since I started TM," Lutz told me one afternoon in Philadelphia. "But I don't feel as bad when I lose."

All of which brings us back to Tim Gallwey's Inner Game theories. His premise is hard to fault: Dissociate the mind from the *implications* of what you're doing and concentration will take care of itself. Gallwey didn't originate the idea. He acknowledges in *The Inner Game of Tennis* that much of what he says about tennis was inspired by Eugen Herrigel, a German philosopher who went to Japan to learn archery from a Zen master and ended up learning about Zen from an archery master. Herrigel's problem, described in a fascinating book called *Zen in the Art of Archery,* is that he was concentrating *too* much, trying *too* hard, getting *too* ego-involved in shooting the arrow.

"Stop thinking about the shot," Herrigel was told at one stage in his training. "That way it is bound to fail. Don't think about what you have to do, or how to carry it out. The shot will only go smoothly when it takes the archer himself by surprise. It must be as if the bowstring suddenly cuts through the thumb that held it. You mustn't open the right hand on purpose."

Eventually, Herrigel learned to dissociate himself from the result of the shot. Which is to say he managed to dispatch Self 1 to some obscure corner of his psyche where it could exercise little, if any, influence on the shot good or bad. Sometimes it broke the rules.

"If ever the least flicker of satisfaction showed in my face, the master turned on me with unwonted fierceness," Herrigel writes. " 'What are you thinking of!' he would cry. 'You already know that you should not grieve over the bad shots; learn now not to rejoice over the good ones. You must free yourself from the buffetings of pleasure and pain, and learn to rise above them in easy equanimity, to rejoice as though not you but another had shot well.' "

Gallwey understood the importance of this concept, but it took him a long time to grasp the message. He had been a good enough tennis player in his teens to win the National Hardcourts championship at fifteen. He had started teaching tennis in the late 1960s after an abortive career as a college administrator, and he went at it in much the same way he'd been taught by his parents: stressing the mechanics. An Army sergeant telling the troops how to dismantle the M-14.

It wasn't until Gallwey launched what he describes as a "personal exploration" into some of the yoga and Zen meditative disciplines of the East that it dawned upon him that there might be a pragmatic connection between certain aspects of Eastern thought and the playing of tennis. "I had always been vaguely aware," Gallwey told me, "that I played my best when I was not conscious of what I was doing; but I was never aware of how big an obstacle it was to playing good tennis when I cared too much about whether or not I hit the ball well, or whether I won or lost." Self 1 revisited. The Vince Lombardi in all of us.

Gallwey:

What we're seeing today in tennis are people who use the game as a means of measuring themselves, and this is a reflection of where our society is. Too many people come to the tennis court with the idea of filling certain psychological holes in their lives. Tennis is supposed to eliminate the feelings of inadequacy. That's why something as simple as missing a stroke takes on greater implications to many people. But what you have to realize is that most errors in tennis occur *because of this very thing. Because we're too caught up in the business of equating self worth with performance, we tighten too many muscles. One of the greatest lessons you can learn from Eastern discipline is that an attachment to the fruits of learning is the greatest barrier to learning.*

When Gallwey elaborates his views, he is so logical and so convincing that it is all you can do to keep from proclaiming, "Amen, brother!" Then you go out and take a short lesson in his driveway and you walk away even more convinced that he is onto something truly revolutionary. For there I was, moments after Gallwey's brief instructions, hitting the best topspin backhands of my life. Zap. Zap. Zap. Each one a picture shot off the backboard. How exhilarating it was. So exhilarating, in fact, that the more I hit well the more nervous I became that I'd miss and break the spell. And when I finally hit a ball that missed the backboard altogether and sailed into the grassy embankment that flanks one side of Gallwey's driveway, I was laughing, but more out of nervousness than out of triumph.

Gallwey was smiling. "You see what happened, didn't you?" he said. "The minute you became conscious of the shots you were hitting and how well you were hitting, you tightened up and missed. It's a very common thing. We are all so accustomed in this culture to the idea of being in conscious control that even when we are performing well, *without* this conscious control, it gets to us. It scares us. But you can train yourself to get out of these feelings."

Gallwey has a satchel filled with stories of people who have reacted to his Inner Game lessons in much the same way I did. One story he tells often concerns a psychotherapist who came to him for a lesson in serving. "This guy had an absolutely terrible serve, but within a half hour I had him serving so beautifully that he was hitting target chairs," Gallwey says. "Well, he came back the next week for a backhand lesson and I asked him about his serve. Sure enough, he'd gone back to his old serve. The way he explained it was he didn't feel comfortable with the new serve. He couldn't understand what was going on, and he couldn't just let it happen. He couldn't allow his Self 1 to stay on the sidelines."

Gallwey has often been accused by more orthodox teaching pros of oversimplifying tennis, of creating the impression that because techniques are unimportant to tennis a teaching pro is superfluous to the learning process.

He says he can understand why some people might take exception to his ideas, and so in his second book, *Inner Tennis,* he went out of his way to clarify some of the basic concepts of his first book:

> *I never meant to give the impression that a Zen master who's never seen a tennis ball can go out on the court for the first time and play like a champion. And I never wanted to give the impression that techniques were unimportant, and that there weren't a lot of physical things you had to master. Ultimately, what I'm saying is that in order for the mind and body to work together, the*

*mind has to be calm and settled—it can't inter-
fere.*

Okay. If you want to concentrate better—by Gallwey's formula—you have to start to forget things instead of trying to remember them. You have to trust
the body, which means taking away the mind's au-
thority. You have to forget about judgments and immerse yourself so completely in the experience at
hand—the ball approaching—that concentration will
happen on its own, without any external prodding.

Does it work? For some people, I'm sure it does.
Certainly, in practice situations, it can work very well
indeed. But a possiible problem with Gallwey's theories,
as Vic Braden has pointed out a number of times, is
that in order to put them into play, you have to alter
not only your way of thinking on a tennis court but
your way of thinking per se. "You have to get into
another world," says Braden. "You can't look at the
world one way off the court and another way on the
court."

I myself have tried on many occasions to institute
some of Gallwey's suggestions, which is to say I have
tried not to try. After I came back from California, I
got into the habit of reading through *The Inner Game
of Tennis* a couple of times a week, and soon I was
playing tennis with a lot of his concepts in mind. In a
way, it worked. Whenever I'd find myself getting anxious or becoming too judgmental, I'd slip Self 1 a
quarter to get lost, and then, with Self 2 at the controls,
I'd hit some dandy shots.

And that's where "the problem" came in. As soon as
I'd hit a couple of great shots, Self 1 would somehow get
wind of it; in an effort to show Self 1 that I could repeat

the performance *without* his help, I would try to duplicate the feat—not realizing at the time, of course, that I was playing right into Self 1's hands. Once I realized I was back to trying again, I would try to stop—until I discovered that trying *not* to try is as bad as trying! By this time, my head would be so mixed up, I'd curse the day I ever heard of Tim Gallwey.

It's probably my fault. Deep down I have no doubt that Gallwey is absolutely correct when he brands the judgmental, conscious Self 1 as the true villain of our individual tennis dramas. If we could somehow immerse ourselves so completely in the immediate task at hand—hitting the tennis ball—and not bring to it so much psychic baggage in the form of desire, anxiety and compulsion, our performance would indeed take on a remarkable new dimension. But what then? What about the next time we play?

There is, I'm sure, an answer to this dilemma, but I don't think I'll ever find it on the tennis court. Tim Gallwey, I suspect, would agree.

2

Emotions on the Court: The Mind at War

People always say to me that if I not do what I do on the court when I get upset then I will be a much better player, but I can't stop it. That's me. That's my game. I don't know. Sometimes I think I love tennis too much. If I don't get excited, then it's not me.

ILIE NASTASE

THE pros call it "the elbow," short for "steel elbow." It has happened to me so many times it is depressing even to mention it. A point or two away from victory, I ease to the net behind an approach shot that forces so fat and so feeble a return that a simple block volley—a shot I can make with my eyes closed in the warm-up—will win the point. Except that somewhere in the course of the swing, as if struck by instant paralysis, my arm refuses to do what it knows how to do, and what it is supposed to do. The dismal, soul-wrenching result is a volley that plummets into the net or sails a foot beyond the sideline. There's no getting around it: steel elbow has struck. I have "choked" again.

Choking. It's a messy subject no matter how you approach it. Bring the matter up in the company of tennis professionals and most become noticeably reticent. Republican Party fundraisers at the mention of Watergate. Everyone is willing to admit that an attack of nerves can produce nightmarish results on a tennis court, but few people really understand why. And fewer still are comfortable discussing the subject, especially in terms of themselves. You'd do better pumping a Green Beret sergeant about combat fatigue.

Part of the problem here, of course, is the stigma that surrounds the inability to keep your nerves and emotions laid back in pressure situations, as if choking on a tennis court were tantamount to the desertion of a mugging victim. When the going gets tough, after all, the tough are supposed to get going. Dependable in the clutch, and, thanks, Vince Lombardi, I needed that.

Would that it were all that black and white: a matter of separating the men from the boys. It's not. Virtually everybody who plays tennis is obliged to wage his own private war with his nerves and emotions. So the question isn't who does or doesn't choke or who does or doesn't lose his temper. It's the degree to which these outbursts affect different players. Rod Laver can isolate any number of occasions in his career when pressure temporarily got to him. Serving for match point against Roy Emerson at Forest Hills the first time he won the Grand Slam in 1962, for instance, Laver was so clutched he had the racquet turned wrong on the ensuing volley and hit the ball straight down at his feet.

The normally smooth serving Charlie Pasarell, down a set point in a Davis Cup match, once tightened up so badly that he hit the ball on the frame and knocked it into the stadium seats. John Newcombe, whom many people consider one of the best pressure players in the history of the game, once double faulted twice in a row in the final game of the fifth set in a Forest Hills match against Tony Roche. And, in the opinion of many players on the tour, including Arthur Ashe, Jimmy Connors choked badly the year he lost to Ashe in the finals of Wimbledon.

I make these observations with deference. What is noteworthy about the players just mentioned is not that they have faltered on occasion in the pinch but that these lapses have happened—and happen—with such relative infrequency. For whatever differences there may be between world class players and that immense army of second level players whose names you will never see in tennis magazines, none is more crucial than the ability to hang tough in pressure situations.

Charlie Pasarell:

I can think of dozens of players that nobody has ever heard about who can hit the ball as well and as hard as anybody on the tour but just can't get it together in a match situation. The reason that guys like Laver and Newcombe and Connors are champions is that they always do their best on big points in key situations. Most players, on a big point, will play it safe, let the other guy make the error. But the great players aren't afraid to gamble. They'll choke, too, every now and then, but usually they're going to put the pressure on you.

What exactly is it that differentiates a Laver or a Newcombe or a Connors, not to mention a King or an Evert or a Borg or any other champion, from players in whom the pressure invariably brings out something less than their best? Is it something innate or something learned? How much is playing well under pressure related to the technical ability, and to what degree are the better pressure players consciously aware of the forces that put them in a special category? I don't pretend to have definitive answers to all of these questions but neither am I willing to concede that the answers lie hidden within some mystical power that defies analysis and understanding. There are reasons why pressure affects different players in different ways and why certain players are somehow able to *raise* the level of their game in pressure situations. But before we can get any sort of handle on these reasons, we have to first clarify a larger question: how emotions in general relate to the physical and technical demands of not just tennis but of any physical activity.

THE ANATOMY OF AN EMOTION

THE emotions represent an area of mental activity about which psychologists and physiologists are very much in the dark. Even defining the term poses a problem. On the one hand, an emotion is a subjective feeling—pity, anger, love, hate, disgust. On the other hand, it's a pattern of internal responses with a profound effect upon the body's behavioral machinery. While you're *feeling* angry, things are happening inside that will enable you to *act* angry. Ever since researchers began looking into the neural and physiological bases of emotion in the 1890s there has been a debate over whether "feelings" trigger the internal responses or vice versa. The prevailing theory today is one that combines the two points of view. A stimulus appears to ignite a general level of emotional arousal but no specific feeling. Not until the brain has had an opportunity to appraise the situation and trigger the appropriate signals does the feeling become more specific. Presumably, there are chemicals in the body that interact with the nervous system in ways that produce what we experience as specific emotions. But what these chemicals are and how they are triggered is an open question.

Much less of an open question is what happens to the body when the mind gets itself into a state of emotional arousal. The body is a self-governing machine with a remarkable capacity to adjust its energy production according to the demands that get placed upon it. Subject the body to any sort of arousal, be it physical or psychological, and certain internal events take place automatically. The first thing that happens is that the adrenal glands, on a signal from the brain, start pumping additional adrenaline into the bloodstream. Whoosh! Like a slave master's whip, adrenaline has the effect of speeding everything up. Heart rate intensifies. Blood pressure rises. Whatever glucose is available in the body is rerouted from the skin and internal organs to those muscle groups that support what anthropologists like to call "flight or fight" behavior. The body, in short, is preparing for war.

But nature giveth and nature taketh away. The muscles that benefit from this arousal once it becomes intense are the muscle groups most involved with so-called "flight or fight" behavior—the heart, for instance, and the muscles that support large scale physical activities, like running, or lifting or pulling. Sacrificed during this exercise are the muscles and nerves that control delicate and precise motor activities. Tying a shoelace. Threading a needle. Playing the piano. The reason it works this way is logical. Thousands of generations of human evolution have proven that if you are being chased down an alley by a couple of Neanderthals, it is better to run like O. J. Simpson than play piano like Arthur Rubinstein.

All in all, it's not a bad system—except for one thing. What if you want to thread a needle, tie a shoelace or play the piano and the mind is behaving as if you were being chased down an alley by a couple of Neanderthals? Why should the mind behave thusly? Mainly because a big part of the mind's job is not only to respond to danger but to *anticipate* it. Frequently it goes overboard. It is 3 a.m. and the ringing of the phone jars you awake. What would you do if you were the mind and the phone rang at 3 a.m.? You would sound an alarm, of course. Flood the system with adrenaline. And if the call turns out to be a wrong number—well, *c'est la vie*. Better cautious than dead. In the meantime, however, the neural troops have all donned their battle gear. Sleep, for the time being, is out of the question.

Which brings us to tennis. In some respects, the phone is always ringing at 3 a.m. on a tennis court. That is to say, the mind is forever priming the body for responses that frequently have no place in tennis combat. Tennis is a sport requiring a combination of coordination, precision, quickness, clear thinking, and concentration, not to mention a healthy lung capacity. A certain amount of adrenaline is indispensable to fuel these activities, much like a dollop or two of tabasco sauce puts the blood in a bloody mary. But an excess of adrenaline can—and usually does—generate a state of hyper-arousal that makes it difficult to meet the game's more specific requirements.

A similar dilemma is at work in most sports but there are differences. If your name is Mean Joe Greene and you are richly compensated for the dismantling of other human beings, the more agitation and excitement the better. Adrenaline and aggression are congenial bed-fellows. But if your name is Jack Nicklaus and you are paid to tap a small ball into a small hole, the last thing you need is a surplus of behavioral juice.

The problem with tennis is that it asks you to be part Joe Greene and part Jack Nicklaus. The overall physical demands of the game—the running and the quickness and need for sharp reflexes—create a need for a healthy level of arousal. But if the arousal gets out of hand, the phone starts to ring at 3 a.m. and the precise demands of the game lose out.

There's another factor involved here as well. If it were only the *physical* demands of the game that the mind had to deal with, the delicate adrenaline balancing act that is a prerequisite for successful playing could probably be handled by most players. There is, after all, a stop and go rhythm to tennis, opportunities to catch your breath and clear your head. But the mind has other things to concern itself with—namely, the *mental* pressures of the game.

And mental pressures there are—in abundance. The fact that the brain is being called upon to marshal a series of rather specific responses every few seconds is pressure inducing. The fact that these responses have to be made in a one-on-one, competitive situation is pressure inducing. The fact that the inability to make these responses can generate frustration and anger is pressure inducing.

There's more: the added pressure we bring upon ourselves when we introduce to the tennis playing situation implications which involve not the game itself but, rather, the significance we attach to it. Technically speaking, it is no more difficult to produce a down the line backhand at match point in the Wimbledon finals than it is to produce the same shot if you're working out on a ball machine on a local court, but the *actual* difficulty factor between the two can only be measured in light years. Julie Heldman once described her own mental struggles with tennis as "a constant battle to trick myself into thinking that it didn't matter." She adds that she was rarely successful at it. And Bob Lutz summarizes the feelings of nearly every professional player I've ever spoken with.

Lutz:

You do your best to keep telling yourself that a match is just another match and a point is just another point, but the realization always seems to creep in anyway. When you're a point or two away from winning, it's very difficult to convince yourself that it's just another point. How do you get yourself to believe what is, isn't?

How, indeed? Asking the brain *not* to anticipate the excitement of a big win, or *not* to sound the alarm when it senses that you're about to lose control of a situation you desperately want to keep control of is like asking for a rewrite of evolutionary history. Originally a hunter, man, remember, was not to the tennis court born. Our gut responses are better suited to the jungle than to the tennis court. Shoot first, ask questions later.

Not that I'm trying to paint a hopeless picture. To say that tennis presents the mind with barriers it is not inherently equipped to overcome is not to say these barriers are insurmountable. Many players—the more successful players, to be sure—have learned to manage the emotional and mental pressures of the game in ways that minimize, if not entirely eliminate, the choking reactions that are more or less endemic to the game. And while the methods used by these players are different, the approach has generally been the same. What the more successful tennis players have learned to do is to control the most volatile—but also the most controllable—agent in the choking process: anxiety. I'll get to *how* some of these players do this later in the chapter. For now, though, let's have a look at anxiety itself the better to see just what produces it and what damage it creates on the tennis court.

THE ANATOMY OF ANXIETY

BECAUSE it is a subject unto itself, I don't intend to get too deeply immersed in the dynamics of anxiety, except to clarify the role it plays in determining the level of inner excitement on the loose in the body at any given moment in a tennis match. We've already established that the mind has its own method of monitoring the energy demands of the body, and that the inherent nature of tennis creates arousal in its own right. So, things being how they are, the mind could get along very nicely, thank you, without the additional arousal kicked up by anxiety. Anxiety only serves to increase what is already an almost overflowing stream of adrenaline. With friends like anxiety, the mind does not need enemies.

That a sport in which the danger of physical injury is slight should generate anxiety may seem illogical on the surface. But tennis produces anxiety because players attach to it a symbolic meaning that transcends the tennis court. "It comes about," Julie Anthony says, "when we begin to evaluate who we are with what we do on the tennis court."

In the professional game, of course, anxiety has understandable roots. There is generally something tangible at stake, apart from winning itself, whenever a professional tennis player competes.

Cliff Drysdale:

If your livelihood depends on your ability to win tennis matches, there is always a little of yourself on the line every time you go out on a court. Winning has the effect, symbolically, of making everything easier for you and your family years in the future. Losing has the opposite effect.

The event, the amount of money at stake, the setting, the opponent—all of these things affect the anxiety level of professional players in different ways. Wimbledon, because of its historical significance and its prestige (not to mention the economic benefits that accrue to its champions), almost invariably spikes the anxiety level in most players—so much so that Sherwood Stewart recalls that the first time he served at Centre Court at Wimbledon, he missed the toss entirely. Davis Cup competition is, for most players, a much more emotionally trying experience than regular tournament play. "What does it," says Tony Trabert, "is the realization that you're not playing for yourself but for millions of people." Playing in front of a hometown crowd is a problem for many players, among them Manuel Orantes, who reports that while he can deal with his own disappointment when he's not playing well, he can't deal with the disappointment of his countrymen. And it has only been recently that Chris Evert has been able to take the court against Evonne Goolagong without experiencing a nervous stirring that is noticeably absent when she plays everybody else.

Then there are the idiosyncratic anxiety patterns that characterize many players. Virginia Wade, for instance, admits that the nervousness she experiences on a tennis court is related not so much to whether she wins or loses but to how she looks doing it. Linky Boshoff says she has no anxiety about losing but does worry, on occasion, about being humiliated on the court. Cliff Drysdale admits that there are one or two players on the tour with whom his personal relations are so strained that he invariably tightens up. And Gene Scott says that when he was competing, he was always more anxious when he was playing somebody that he felt he *should* beat than when he was playing someone who was a notch or two better than he was.

Scott:

It's a common reaction among some players. If you're up against a top player, you figure you have nothing to lose by losing and so you don't worry about it. But if you're playing somebody you figure you should beat, then you have to deal with how you're going to feel about yourself in the event you do lose.

It needn't be stressed that the presence—or absence—of anxiety in a tennis situation is very much related to personality. How you feel about yourself, how important—or unimportant—it is for you to win, how excitable you are in general: it all affects the kind of responses you will make under pressure. And let us not forget the importance of basic talent in this process. Ilie Nastase, by his own admission, is almost always anxious in big matches, but his talent reservoir is so vast that the effects are not as costly to him as they would be to a less nervous, but less talented player, like, say, Harold Solomon. For the bottom line, remember, is not so much what sort of nervous reactions you're having on the court but the effect these reactions are having on your game.

But is there a substantial difference in the anxiety levels of professional players? You bet! But the differences are not always easy to discern. First of all, you can't always pinpoint anxiety as the culprit behind a technical lapse that occurs in a pressure situation. Harry Hopman notes that players who appear to be choking are often being victimized by a favorite stroke that happens to have a small margin for error. Roy Emerson's tendency to choke, Hopman points out, disappeared almost overnight once Emmo began to hit his forehand with more topspin, making it a safer shot. Hopman also defends the rash of double faults that cost Dennis Ralston a victory over Rod Laver in the 1969 U.S. Open Championships at Forest Hills.

Hopman:

Ralston was a prime example of a player who had a shot that left little margin for error. It was his service. At Ralston's peak, he possessed a serve

*that barely skimmed the net and struck deep, al-
most on the service box line. But when he tried to
do more with it, there was no room for improve-
ment, only room for error.*

Billy Talbert:

*Everybody has what I like to call a choking margin.
There were certain strokes in my game—my return of serve, or my backhand—that I never worried about choking on because I felt so comfortable
with these shots. Even if I did tighten just a little,
I still had plenty of safety margin. But then I'd
get out there against a guy like Don Budge, who
was so sound in every way, and I knew I had to
make perfect shots in order to win points. I didn't
have that ability, and so I missed. It wasn't a question of choking, it was a question of trying to do
what I knew I had to do if I wanted to win—and
then not being able to do it.*

Another thing. You don't necessarily have to *tighten
up* to choke. The symptoms of anxiety vary widely from
player to player. Fred McNair says he gets slightly dizzy
when he's nervous. Rod Laver experiences a vague
sense of remoteness, as if he'd just been dropped into a
hostile environment. Margaret Court loses her timing.
And Arthur Ashe has trouble breathing.

Ashe, from *Portrait in Motion:*

*I may never look like I'm choking, but that can be
very misleading. Right now, when I'm nervous on
the court, I have actual difficulty in breathing. And
the problem is compounded when I try to run. My
legs move stiffly, and soon my whole body offers
only the most deliberate movements. It's as if I've*

lost all my instincts for playing tennis, so that my
mind must try to explain repeatedly to my body
what it already knows how to do.

Few professionals have ever described choking reactions more candidly than Ashe, but it would be
wrong to conclude that Ashe is any more susceptible
to choking than other players on the tour. Ashe points
out, for instance, that many "calm" players choke in
their own manner.

Ashe:

A guy can be calm and cool on the court and still
be choking. Maybe he's resigned himself to losing,
which, to me, is a choke. Maybe he didn't train the
way he should have for the match. Maybe he didn't
go to bed early the night before. When you come
down to it, anything you do to give yourself a rea-
son for losing is a choke.

Something else, too. The choking of many players
frequently goes unnoticed by tennis spectators. Instead
of committing glaring errors—a double fault at a key
point—certain players will, in certain situations, shift
their games into a lower gear. Their groundstrokes
won't go out but they won't land as deep. Their volleys
will lose their customary bite. Their serves will land
more shallow than usual. Stan Smith once told me that
even when Rod Laver was playing his best tennis, you
could tell when he was getting a little nervous because
he would start to chip his backhand. Roy Emerson remembers that in the early 1960s some of his opponents
would sense his anxiousness through his tendency to
rush in between points. "What a lot of players started

doing," Emmo says, "was to deliberately stall, and this made me more anxious."

Yet there are—and have been—professional players for whom anxiety, in most instances, is simply not a problem. Ham Richardson, a top rated amateur player in the 1950s, is one example.

Richardson:

The only time I can ever remember nerves really getting to me in a match was when I was eighteen and playing in Europe. I managed to beat my opponent but not until I'd lost my serve three times in a row. It might have been the unfamiliar surroundings—I don't know. I do know that I always went into a match with a pretty realistic idea of how I fared compared with the other player. I never cared that much about being the best player in the world, so I was mainly concerned with doing what I could do best. And if I won, so much the better.

I mention Richardson specifically here because his sentiments call to mind some of the attitudes exemplified by contemporary players who are judged by their colleagues as being fairly immune to the consequences of anxiety on the court. I'm thinking in particular of players like Bjorn Borg, Harold Solomon, Chris Evert, Evonne Goolagong, and Sue Barker, all of whom seem notably less prone to nervousness than the average touring pro and all of whom bring to the court, apart from everything, an attitude untainted by the fear of losing.

Goolagong, in particular, takes winning and losing remarkably in stride, insisting that she can be this way only because she "enjoys the tennis and not the winning." Sue Barker has much the same philosophy. "It's a question," she says, "of really enjoying what you do. If you're enjoying yourself, then you're not worried about how well or badly you're doing." And Chris Evert, although she is more competitive and goal-directed than either Goolagong or Barker, insists that a fear of losing has *never* been a factor in her mental attitude.

Evert:

A lot of it really has to do with the way I was raised. My father was very careful to react pretty much the same way whether I won or lost. When he was critical, it was never because of the outcome of the match but because of certain things I may not have done right. But he was never harsh. I never went into a match afraid of how he would react if I lost.

Borg and Solomon have similar points of view—neither enjoys losing but neither overly worries about it—but they have an advantage that other players don't enjoy. Their games are basically defensive and highly physical. Which is another way of saying that if they've trained well enough there isn't too much that can go technically wrong with their strokes. They are Volvos in a world of Porsches. It has been said of Borg that he was so good so young that getting nervous never occurs to him, although there have been defeats in his career that came about not because he was nervous but because he became frustrated and upset and simply stopped trying. A choke, by Arthur Ashe's definition. Solomon's uniqueness, on the other hand, seems to lie in his ability to analyze his defeats logically.

Solomon:

One of the big differences between me and a lot of players is that I really know my strengths and weaknesses. There are very logical reasons why I have trouble with certain players like Borg or Vilas. It's because they're too strong for me to outlast from the baseline, and I'm not sure enough of myself at the net to pressure them. Being worried about it isn't going to help. What I have to do is strengthen my game.

Being able to view yourself objectively and to take your lumps philosophically are useful traits to have no matter what your line of work is but there is a fine line between having a realistic appreciation of your own capabilities and underestimating yourself. Butch Buchholz is one former player who admits that he was never able to view his losses within a logical framework, yet, feels that he was a more successful player because of it.

Buchholz:

Looking back, I can see that I kidded myself a great deal because there were weaknesses in my game that I refused to acknowledge. I took my defeats hard because I couldn't understand how I could lose. But on the other hand, I probably won a lot of matches I wouldn't have otherwise won if I hadn't gone in with that attitude.

So much for anxiety as it relates to the professional game. Plenty of choking goes on in recreational tennis, too, never mind that there is rarely anything tangible at stake beyond the outcome of the match.

As Ted Solotaroff, a writer, editor and tennis addict, once put it in a *New York Times Magazine* piece:

My main trouble is not stamina but imagination. Like Henry James, I have the imagination of disaster, which works better for modern literature than it does for tennis. In general, imagination is the neurotic tennis player's substitute for concentration. Concentration means that you are following a clearcut set of orders: "Move to the ball, get your racquet back, set your feet, see the ball, squeeze the handle, stride, see the ball meet the racket, follow through," and so forth. But my imagination can't be bothered with such mundane matters; it's usually too busy adjusting my play to the image I happen to have of myself at the moment. Thus if I have hit a couple of backhand errors in a row, my imagination appears on the scene like a doctor in the house to announce that my backhand has suffered a relapse, and my following strokes will be timid with dismay and caution. I have just hit a forehand smash down the line in a close match and my opponent has somehow gotten it back, imagination raises the deadening question of what do I have to do to win a point. Or if I am coming in for a weak return, with three-fourths of the court sitting wide open, my imagination will turn grandiose and suggest a really decisive smash or a class drop-shot. This is also known as the death wish.

But why? Why should a perceptive, intelligent man like Solotaroff come apart so on a tennis court? And why should I, for instance, choke in a match against an opponent I know well and like? Why does my game take such a nose-dive if I find myself in a foursome that I'm not especially comfortable with?

I really don't know. Psychologists and psychiatrists I've interviewed tell me that much of the anxiety recreational players experience is rooted in the fear that we will prove ourselves unworthy of the players we're playing with and thus invite the prospect of rejection. I suspect there's more to it. I've noticed in my own circle of partners, for instance, that players who have played a lot of competitive sports as younger men tend to do better under pressure than non-athletes, forgetting for the moment how well they play tennis. Which leads me to theorize that players who are unfamiliar with athletic pressure in general are at a slight disadvantage when it comes to dealing with the pressures of tennis. One of the better competitors on the celebrity tennis circuit, for instance, is actor Jerry Orbach, a pool shark in his youth. "I don't think I hit the ball better than most of the people I play," Orbach says. "But I do know I handle the pressure of competition better."

No matter. Whatever the reasons behind the anxiety —fear of losing, fear of winning, fear of being disgraced, low self-esteem, the need for approval, fear of flying, ad infinitum—the fact remains that it *must* be controlled if you're going to deal effectively with the mental pressures of tennis. A look at how the professionals deal with the problem might give us some insights.

COMING TO GRIPS

LET us retrench. We have already established that the intrinsic physical and mental demands of tennis create the need for a certain amount of inner arousal but that if this arousal gets out of hand the body cannot operate at peak efficiency. We've established, too, that any number of factors—personality, ability, etc.—have a bearing on how well you perform in pressure situations.

What seems to be at work here is a threshold phenomenon—a point at which arousal changes uniforms, switching from ally to saboteur. If the arousal is too far below your threshold, your play will lack the necessary sharpness and intensity. If arousal is *over* the threshold, you may play too tightly and tentatively. Not that it's a fixed point, however. It will vary from player to player and from individual players in different situations.

Here's an illustration of the point I'm trying to make. You are playing the club champion in the first round of your club's singles championship. Nobody, including you, gives you much chance of winning. You normally go into a match with a lot of anxiety about winning, but on this day, because you don't give yourself a chance, you're not worried. You've given anxiety the day off.

Now the match starts and you find yourself concentrating well, hitting the ball crisply, playing each point one at a time—in short, doing all the things the books tell you to do without worrying about whether it's going to work out or not. There is inner arousal, sure, but it is comfortably within your threshold range. You're not choking.

And what happens? Before you know it, you're up 4–0 in the first set and it's your serve. Suddenly it dawns on you that you are not only *in* this match, you have a good shot at winning! Enter the brain. It immediately conjures up an image of what it's going to *mean* to you once word gets out that you've beaten the club's

No. 1 player. Your body, of course, responds to this image. It gets excited. The valve that had controlled your anxiety opens up and—whoosh—Niagara Falls. Your threshold is suddenly swamped. You play the rest of the match like a scarecrow.

I quote from Alvaro Fillol, Jaimie Fillol's brother, after he had lost to Rod Laver in an early round at Forest Hills.

Fillol:

I played well in the beginning of the match, but when I started to win, and I realized who I was playing, I got a little nervous. I just couldn't make the same shots.

Don't be so hard on yourself, Alvaro. There's another side to this threshold business. It has to do with what's going on in the *other* guy's nervous system. Go back to the original situation. Look at it from the club champion's point of view. Because you have never been able to win more than two games a set from him, he is not exactly quivering in his boots at the prospect of playing you. And because his "anxiety of winning" machinery isn't all that operational, his level of inner arousal is well below *his* threshold, too. Probably too low. Consequently, he's not playing with normal consistency, finesse, or power. He's not pressuring you.

It soon dawns upon him that if he doesn't get his act together, he is going to lose to one of the biggest turkeys at the club—a possibility that doesn't please him. His brain conjures up an image, too, and his body reacts to it—but in this case the nervous energy that's released doesn't surpass the threshold, it simply approaches it. As his level of inner arousal increases, so does the proficiency of his strokes. As a result, he begins to play better.

Rod Laver:

I'm the sort of player who needs a challenge if I'm going to play my best. I've always been something of a slow starter, but once I get a little nervous about the possibility of losing, I start to concentrate harder and it gets my game back on track.

Manuel Orantes, after coming from behind to beat Hans Pohlman in an early-round Forest Hills match in 1975:

I won the first set very easily, and in the second set neither one of us was really that serious. We were playing drop shots back and forth and that sort of thing. But pretty soon he won the set, and then he broke my serve in the first game of the third set. There's always the danger of panic in this situation, but I didn't break. I sat down between games and told myself what I had to do to win— how I should play him—and I won the next six games.

The scenario won't always work out this way. Had you and the club champion been more equally matched, and had you been better able to control your inner arousal (and had he controlled his a little less effectively) the stress factor might well have made the difference in the match. For the key to dealing with nerves is not so much to eliminate them from your game but to manage them in a way that works best for your particular threshold level and in that particular situation.

This situational aspect of nerves ought not to be dismissed. Orantes, for instance, is a player whose touch game can be devastated if he becomes too aroused. Even so, he can allow himself more arousal against a player he knows he can beat than against a player who has given him trouble in the past. He can use the arousal more productively in that situation because his threshold level is, presumably, higher than normal.

So it is that on some days, and against some opponents, it will take more (or less) in the way of inner arousal to approach (or exceed) your own particular threshold than on other days and against other opponents. The way you happen to feel physically on a particular day, your frame of mind, your personal feelings about your opponent and whatever subconscious influences may be working on your psyche—any one or all of these things can tip the scales in one direction or the other.

Cliff Richey:

It's a hard thing to explain. On some days, you get out on the court and you can be very keen to win and you'll play super. Other days, you can go out with the same desire, but you don't play with the same abandon.

Yes, it is a hard thing to explain. The main reason is that most of us are unaware of the factors that affect the ever-changing relationship between the threshold level and the arousal level. I once allowed myself to be wired up to a biofeedback machine, which measures what psychologists call GSR—galvanic skin reaction. It's a measurement of inner stress. A dial on the machine went up when the GSR was high and down when it was low. The weird thing about the test was that when it registered higher, I was not consciously aware of any anxiety.

John Newcombe:

I never realized until I worked with a sports psychologist in Australia that there were certain players who were getting to me on a subconscious level. The psychologist would simply mention players' names. Some triggered a bigger response than others, and this surprised me because I wasn't consciously aware that my reactions to these players were any different from my reactions to other players.

Most experienced players have a general grasp of their own stress reaction patterns and have jerry-rigged ways to deal with them. Indeed, most players maintain they *need* this inner excitement to hone their reflexes. "Without these feelings," Chris Evert says, "it's tough to get started. You feel flat and sluggish."

Vic Seixas:

Early in my career I read an article that quoted Ted Williams as saying, "I never overcame nervousness." That statement stuck with me throughout my career. I got to the point where I actully wanted my mouth to feel a little dry. I wanted to be aware of my heart pounding. It gave me the little edge I needed to play my best.

It's important that we not confuse what Seixas describes here and what we might normally think of as nervousness or anxiety. To be nervous before a match is not necessarily to be worried, although the distinction is sometimes difficult to make.

Gardnar Mulloy:

*I was always a little nervous before a match, but
there was nothing specific I was afraid of. It never
entered my mind, for instance, that I would double
fault at a big point. It was more a general feeling.
I'd go out and warm up and think to myself, this
guy is hitting so great, how am I ever going to beat
him. But this was good for me because it really
forced me to look for weakness and develop an idea
of how I should play in order to beat him. Eventually, once I got into the match, I'd stop worrying
about whether I was going to beat him and concentrate on doing the job.*

Fortunately for Mulloy, he could pull off what he's
just described. Most players can't. Most professionals
get rid of their "butterflies" once the match heats up,
but their minds still remain vulnerable to periodic attacks of steel elbow and related miseries. Knowing this,
they have devised their own ways of coping. Wendy
Overton, for instance, has learned that if she doesn't
come down too hard on herself in the beginning when
she misses shots, she doesn't get as nervous as she used
to get early in her career.

Overton:

*The mistake I used to make was to get so angry
with myself as soon as I'd muff a few shots that by
the time the match was halfway through, I was
totally discouraged. Just learning to be nicer to
myself helped my game tremendously.*

Another player with a regrettable tendency to get
down on himself when his shots aren't falling in is

Manuel Orantes. But Orantes has learned in recent years that if he can keep his mind calm and focus on what he has to do to put the other player under pressure, he can keep his nerves under control.

Orantes:

One of the things I've learned about myself is that I can't think about or even watch tennis before a match. What happens when I do this is that I become all stirred up inside. I do my best to keep myself from getting angry and upset. I know as soon as I do that my whole game will fall apart.

For Ingrid Bentzer, letting her mind drift during the break to a subject that has nothing at all to do with tennis ("My little girl, for instance") can often relax her when she feels she's getting too tense for the good of her game. Brian Fairlie is one of many players who advocates deep breathing whenever tension starts to seep in. Billy Talbert says that when he felt himself getting nervous in the middle of a match, he'd try to imagine that he was practicing and he insists it worked most of the time. Tony Roche has a habit of shaking his arm down between points. ("Just to keep it loose.") Marty Riessen will do knee bends or jump up on his toes. "Keep the body loose," he says, "and you can sometimes fool the mind." John Newcombe amends Riessen's theory by suggesting that you smile whenever you feel yourself getting too tense. "It's tough to be tense and to smile at the same time," he says.

If none of these suggestions is of any help to you, you might consider Rod Laver's advice.

Laver:

The thing that has always worked best for me whenever I felt I was getting too tense to play good tennis was to simply remind myself that the worst thing—the very worst thing—that could happen to me was that I'd lose a bloody tennis match. That's all.

Or Arthur Ashe:

The one thing I've learned about tension on the court that's really helped me is something I got from Pancho Gonzales. He told me once that if you can somehow learn to relax in between points, the tension won't build up in a match the way it does if you try to concentrate every second. Just as physical fatigue can make you mentally tired, mental fatigue can get you physically tired. Whatever you do to minimize the tension will make serious choking much less likely.

Fred Stolle:

Forget about the match and the point and the other player and just concentrate on watching the ball. And if you muff a couple of easy shots, learn to shrug them off. You can't tell yourself enough times: it's just a game.

And, finally, a word from Vic Braden:

You have to groove with it. Really. You feel yourself getting all nervous and aroused and the worst thing you can do, really, is fight it because it's gonna surface, anyway. So what you want to do is tell yourself how great it is that you're feeling this excitement. Get used to the feelings. They can't hurt you.

Braden's advice is particularly worth noting because it's the ability to follow it that seems to separate the super great players from the routinely great. Most tennis players deal with their emotions and nerves by keeping them in check. The brain plays the role of jailer. When the tension eventually arises, the result is a more conservative style of play. Choking is taking place but its effects are not great because there is more choking taking place on the other side of the net. Then there are the players who manage to keep their nerves and emotions under control but in a way that enables them to maintain the *same* level of play regardless of the situation. Borg is such a player. So are Chris Evert, Harold Solomon, and Ken Rosewall. Each of these players is known for being able to play the "big points" well but I wonder if we're not being fooled. What seems to happen frequently in big points involving these players is that their opponents are playing the big point poorly.

Not that it makes a difference in the outcome. Borg, for instance, has expressed on many occasions his philosophy for playing big points, which is to keep the pressure on but not to unnecessarily risk an error. His game doesn't *come up* on big points; it just doesn't go down. On occasion he pays the price. Most players who watched the Borg–Connors Forest Hills final in 1976 feel that Borg could have won the tiebreaker in the third set (and probably the match) if he had played more aggressively when Connors faltered and fell behind 2–4. He didn't. If anything, he played a little safer, waiting for Connors to take the initiative, which Connors, of course, did.

Borg:

Against most players, whenever I need only one more point to win the set or to break serve, I can hit the ball fairly shallow because most players will not go for a winner off that shallow shot. They'll tighten up a little, hit the shot safer and give me a chance to win the point on the passing shot. But Connors doesn't play it safe, he just hits out.

Indeed Connors does. For he is one of those athletes blessed with the ability to *lift* the level of his game when confronted with pressure. Gonzales could do it. So could Laver in his prime. And Newcombe. And Billie Jean King. Granted, each of these players has extraordinary ability, but there is a special dimension to this ability—a dimension that can be called, for lack of a better term, confidence.

ANTIDOTE TO NERVES: CONFIDENCE

WHAT penicillin is to pneumonia, confidence is to the choke. If you are confident—*genuinely* confident —the sequence of psychological and physical events that produces choking on the court is simply not going to happen frequently enough to make a negative difference in your tennis. You will choke on occasion, like everyone else, but you will do it less than most—and rarely when it really counts.

But how do we define a concept as vague and as fleeting as confidence? More importantly, how do we get a real handle on it?

Roy Emerson:

The whole thing is to have a positive mental approach. You can see it in a player like Newcombe. When Newcombe is serving well, you can feel the confidence across the other side of the net. He's not worried about the ball going in: he's just blasting away. The worst thing you can do on a court is to say to yourself: "Do I hit this serve with everything I have, or do I have to get it in?" You can't think in these terms. You have to make up your mind that you're going to hit the bloody serve and go ahead and hit it.

Okay, that *describes* confidence, but we still haven't pinned it down. Confidence is basically nothing more than a feeling—a belief that you can do a particular thing—but it shares with concentration a frustrating elusivity. You can be confident one moment and bereft of confidence the next. You can be confident in one set of circumstances and not in another. Roscoe Tanner, for obvious reasons, feels more confident on a fast surface that adds thunder to his serve than on a slow surface. Eddie Dibbs feels more confident on clay than he does on asphalt. It depends a lot on whom you're playing, too. Marty Riessen, for example, suggests that a big reason American players tended to do better against Rod Laver in Laver's prime than Australian players was that Americans weren't as overwhelmed by the *idea* of playing Laver. "It always seemed to me," Reissen says, "that most of the Australians conceded defeat even before the match started."

Let's not overstate the case. In and of itself, confidence is not a form of behavior. Only when it is overlaid with some specific activity does it make its presence noticed. And even then, it can take you only as far as you are physically and technically capable of going. The most confident runner in the world isn't going to do a mile in four minutes if the lung capacity isn't there. The most "confident" tennis player isn't going to get very far if he spends too much time getting his head into gear and too little time on his tennis game.

But what confidence *can* do is eliminate mental barriers that prevent you from performing to the outer limits of your capability. There is probably a finite limit to how well you can play on any day *with* confidence, but there is no limit to how poorly you can play if you lack it.

Brian Gottfried:

The difference between feeling confident when you're playing and not feeling confident is that you never hesitate to go for shots and you're not giving your opponent the extra opportunities you give him when you're not feeling confident and you're just trying to keep the ball in play.

Stan Smith:

When you're not confident, it affects nearly everything you do on the court: the way you move, the way you hit the ball, the way you think. You let winning opportunities go by, you tighten up on easy points. It's the catalyst to your entire game. When it goes, your game goes.

Gottfried and Smith, of course, are talking in absolute terms. As Dennis Ralston reminds us, confidence can be as elusive as concentration, even more so.

Ralston:

It comes and goes in a match. You can serve a game and have a feeling that you can close your eyes and get every first serve in. Ten minutes later, you've lost it and you're worrying about losing the game on double faults.

Confidence feeds upon itself. A series of events seem to take place within the brain at one minute that determines how you will feel about the same series of events two or three minutes from now—or even two or three weeks from now. Perhaps in anticipation of the remarkable potential for self-deception that exists within the human spirit, the brain appears to have been endowed with its own accounting system. When the time comes to make a judgment on whether you will or won't succeed in a particular task, promises and salesmanship will only go so far. If you have double faulted each of the past three service games at game point, the next time there's a game point there is very little you can do to persuade the brain that it doesn't have anything to worry about *this* time.

Julie Anthony:

My feeling about confidence is that if you've got one big shot you can really count on, it tends to carry over to the rest of your game. One of the reasons I think there are more genuinely confident men players than women players is that a lot of men players have tremendous confidence in their serves. So when the serve is working, they figure the worst they can do is stay even. Most women don't have that luxury.

Not that the brain isn't receptive to a logical, well presented argument. Two weeks after he beat Jimmy Connors in the finals of the 1976 North American Zone Davis Cup finals, Raul Ramirez admitted that before the competition began he did not feel very confident about his chances. By the time he took the court against Connors in the finals, however, his mental attitude had changed.

Ramirez:

A very strange thing happened. Even though I didn't give myself much of a chance against Connors, when the newspaper reporters and everyone asked me what was going to happen (if it came down to Connors and me in the final) I had to tell them that, of course, I thought I was going to win. So they started asking me why, and I started to think up reasons. And the more I thought about the reasons—especially the fact that I had Davis Cup experience and Jimmy didn't—the more I began to realize that I really was going to win. And when I finally went out on the court, I was very confident.

Call it psycho-cybernetics, if you will: when you have a mental block about something, sit down and list all the reasons the mental block shouldn't be there. It can work—providing, you are able to mount a strong argument.

But in many situations where mental blocks exist, the mind is resistant to change, often unreasonably so.

Here it's been at least six months since you've double faulted at a big point, and now you find yourself suddenly starting to worry about it. Try to explain to the brain that what happened six months ago is past history. The brain is likely to remind you that history has a habit of repeating itself. It will even show you film clips.

Richey:

I once lost a match to Sandy Mayer when I double faulted at game point at 5–3 in the final set. Months later, whenever I'd find myself in that same situation—where I was ahead in a close match on my serve—I'd think back to that point, and I'd worry about it. This is not the way to win tennis matches.

Laver:

You get into winning or losing patterns. A lot of it's getting the breaks. If you win a lot of close matches, your attitude when you get into close matches is, "No sweat, I've been here before and I'll be here again." But if you start to lose a lot of close ones, or you get ahead in a match, then the whole picture changes. The other guy starts to catch up and you start to think, "Oh, oh, here it comes again." Basically, I think this is what happened to Stan Smith. He lost just enough of the edge so that the close ones he used to win he began losing, and that changed his entire attitude about his game.

Many players have trouble keeping negative influences from infiltrating the mind. If Virginia Wade isn't hitting the ball smoothly, she'll get impatient with herself even if she's well ahead, a trait shared by any number of players for whom looking good on a tennis court is as important as winning. Players who play very controlled tactical styles are often thrown off when the unexpected happens.

Anthony:

Certain players have an idea in their minds that tennis is a very logical game, and that if you do A, B, and C, then X, Y, and Z will happen. Usually, it will work out this way, but there's a random element to tennis, too, and certain players simply cannot cope when the predictable things don't happen. This is why I say that thinking too much on the court can get you into trouble.

If the brain does indeed base its judgments on past performance, it's logical to wonder why it doesn't use as a frame of reference one's *good* days and ignore the bad days? A capital suggestion, except for one thing: negative experiences in most cases seem to make a stronger impression than positive experiences, rather like a bank that is more curious about the time you went bankrupt than the ten times you created a successful business. Ultimately, negative experiences create a fallout whose residue appears to seep into the subconscious.

The presence of these negative memory tapes deep within the subconscious is probably the principal barrier to a feeling of *genuine* confidence. The problem is, you can't really get to these memory banks through conventional means. Often, the minute your conscious mind tampers with the brain's memory bank, the brain rejects the new data—without your consent or awareness.

There seems to be two solutions to this dilemma. One is to stockpile a succession of positive experiences which, by their sheer weight, eventually work their way past the brain into the subconscious. There they can eradicate the negative tapes, or at least quiet them down. "I'm winning now because I'm confident," Brian Gottfried said in the midst of his hot streak during the early part of 1977. "But the reason I'm confident is that I'm winning." Torben Ulrich has a habit of slowly going through the motions of a stroke two or three times after he has made an error. "All the bad habits you accumulate in your life never leave you," he explains, "and sometimes, without any real reason, they'll surface. What you have to do is put them back in their place by grafting the proper habits over them."

The second solution to the dilemma, and a more adventurous one, is to go right to the core of it. You circumvent the brain altogether in order to *reprogram the subconscious*—i.e., you undergo hypnosis or a related experience. More athletes than you might imagine have sought the help of hypnotists to restore confidence. One such resource is a Los Angeles man named Arthur Ellen, whose subjects have included hundreds of prominent performers and athletes, among them Harry Belafonte, Jackie Jensen, Maury Wills, Don Sutton, and, reportedly (no one will say for certain), Stan Smith. Ellen contends that when an athlete goes into a slump, the reasons are nearly always subconscious in origin.

Hypnosis, Ellen is careful to point out, cannot imbue you with physical skills you do not already possess.

Ellen:

If an athlete doesn't have the skills to begin with,
hypnosis isn't going to help. Where hypnosis does
help is in getting directly into the subconscious
to eliminate the blocks that have been formed.
The purpose of hypnosis is to help the athlete be
as good as he can be; he shouldn't be held back by
fears and concerns that aren't really connected
with what he already knows how to do. What I
try to develop with troubled athletes is an im-
munity *to anxiety. It's really a relearning pro-*
cess. They've "learned" to be afraid and to doubt
themselves. Under hypnosis, we can circumvent
that negative learning and then, by means of
post-hypnotic suggestion, teach them how to use
the "new" learning whenever they feel the anxiety
coming on.

I liked what Ellen said. If I had been a Californian, I
would have gone to see him. Instead, I went to see a
hypnotist in Monroe, Connecticut. He was not a hypnotist, exactly. That is, he *used* to be a hypnotist before
he became something else: a faith healer. Although
this discovery was somewhat disconcerting, I heard the
man out, anyway. He agreed with nearly everything
Arthur Ellen had said—that we do, in fact, create our
own mental barriers. And even though he didn't know
much about tennis, he could certainly understand how
such mental barriers would interfere with performance. But he disagreed strongly with Ellen on how to
eliminate these mental barriers.

"Hypnosis can work," he said, "but just about anyone who is capable of being hypnotized is capable of doing the same thing on his own."

At first, I was skeptical, but I listened anyway; and the more I listened, the more fascinated I became. The mind, he told me, is an incredibly powerful instrument that can be programmed to develop whatever image we wish. It's simply a matter of feeding the mind strictly positive inputs. "Everything we do in life," he explained, "makes an impact one way or the other on the mind and on the image we have of ourselves. But people can control that image much more than they think."

I wanted some specifics. How do you get the mind to view in a positive manner four consecutive double faults?

"You act as though they never happened," he said.

"But they *did* happen," I said. "Otherwise the guy wouldn't have lost his serve at love."

"Which guy?" he asked.

"The guy who double faulted," I said.

"Maybe it didn't happen to him," he suggested.

"What do you mean, *maybe*?" I asked. "It *happened*."

"You don't understand," he said. "Maybe it didn't happen to *him*?"

"To who," I asked.

"To *him*," he said.

I was confused.

"Look," he explained. "If I were a tennis player, which I'm not, I would go into every match, every game and every point with an image of myself as a player who never made a bad shot—*never*."

"The perfect tennis player," I said.

"Exactly."

"But there is no such thing," I insisted.

"You're wrong," he said. "I am. You are."

"Me?" Now I was really getting worried. "Look," I said. "A perfect tennis player is an illusion, for one thing. And for another, there's no way in the world I could ever convince myself that I was close to being a perfect tennis player."

He smiled indulgently. "But let's say, for the sake of argument, that you *were* the perfect tennis player. "Would the Perfect Tennis Player ever make mistakes?"

"No," I said.

"And if he never made mistakes, would he ever worry about making them?"

"No."

"That's right. That's why you should go out on a tennis court with the idea in your mind that you're perfect."

"But what about the double faults?" I asked. "What does the perfect tennis player say to himself after he has double faulted?"

I thought I had him. I didn't.

"He doesn't say anything to himself, because it didn't happen to him."

"What do you mean, it *didn't* happen?" I persisted.

"How could it have happened," the faith-healer replied, "if the man was the perfect tennis player?"

Now I began to get the picture, and I liked what I saw. For what if you could indeed convince yourself *before* every point that you were the perfect tennis player, regardless of what happened on the previous point? What would happen then? I'll tell you—*you wouldn't choke*. You couldn't choke, because perfect tennis players don't do that. Sure, you might miss the shot, but you could always tell yourself that it didn't happen to *you,* because it couldn't have happened to a perfect player.

On the same afternoon that I had this conversation, I played tennis with a good player whom I'd never beaten. "I am the perfect tennis player," I said to myself as I warmed up. I missed a few shots in the warm-up, but I ignored them. After all, they didn't happen to me. They couldn't have.

It almost worked. I say almost because I played noticeably better than I usually play. I wasn't getting down on myself whenever I blew an easy shot. Early in the first set, I double faulted. Correction: Somebody else double faulted—someone less perfect than I.

The curious part is that my brain was going along with the whole thing. Oh, I may have detected a snicker or two when a "perfect player" drop volley I tried landed five feet out. But, all in all, it was letting me alone. It wasn't interfering.

"It won't interfere," the faith-healer had said "as long as you don't take a negative approach. The brain will comply as long as you stay positive, but the minute you tell yourself that you're *not* going to do something —that you're not going to get nervous, or you're *not* going to double fault—then you're telling the brain that you're not perfect. And you can't tell yourself you're perfect and *not* tell yourself you're perfect at the same time."

For a while, everything worked terrific. The only thing that surprised me was that a perfect tennis player should have lost the first set 6–4. But that's the point, isn't it, to be surprised when defeat happens? That's what confidence is. Midway through the second set, I began to sense a certain impatience in certain sectors of my brain. I think it happened in the third game when I double faulted twice in a row. Since my brain had apparently taken a sudden interest in who won the match, it would have preferred, I think, that I ease up a little on the second serve. Perfect players, I tried to explain, don't do that sort of thing. Seconds later, at game point, I double faulted again, and it was at this point that my brain decided it had had quite enough of this "perfect player" nonsense. I heard the vault to my subconscious shut with an authoritative clang. "You had your chance," my brain seemed to say. "And you blew it."

I accepted the decision, but I haven't given up. I still have Arthur Ellen's number on file.

Do you want to know a *real* perfect player? I'll tell you: it's Jimmy Connors. Whether he knows it or not, Connors puts into practice everything the faith-healer hypnotist talked about. There is no more confident player in tennis. And the remarkable thing about Connors is that he has always been this way, even as a young rising star when he was losing to players like Van Dillen and Solomon.

"We knew from the beginning that Jimmy was going to be the greatest player in the world," Jimmy Connors's mother, Gloria, once told me. "So we—Jimmy's grandmother and I—taught him the sort of game he could grow into. We taught him to hit out on the big points, never to hold back, because that's the only way to become a champion."

Teenagers who go for the bleachers on every point usually lose in the second or third round to young pushers who keep the ball in play. They are also likely to end up life as tennis-playing dentists. Many of these teenagers, moreover, never recover from the losing habit and eventually give up tennis altogether.

It didn't happen to Connors, though, because no one *let* it happen. For it wasn't young Connors who lost those matches in which the other players had the higher score. Perfect players, remember, don't lose.

"If it weren't for my mom and grandmother," Connors has said on many occasions, "I could never have made it. They were so sensational in their support, they never allowed me to lose confidence. They just kept telling me to play the same way, and they kept assuring me that it would eventually come together. And I believed them."

He still does. The day before Jimmy Connors beat Bjorn Borg in the finals of the 1976 U.S. Open at Forest Hills, he was talking in the locker room about confidence. Had I closed my eyes I might have been back with my faith-healer.

Connors:

The whole thing is never to get negative about yourself. Sure, it's possible that the other guy you're playing is tough, and that he may have beaten you the last time you played, and, okay, maybe you haven't been playing all that well yourself. But the minute you start thinking about these things, you're dead. I go out to every match convinced that I'm going to win. That is all there is to it.

3

Tactics

When I was a young player, I never really thought about tennis strategy except for the basic things, like when to go to net and things like that. But then I started working with Lew Hoad who made me realize that if you understand your own game and your opponent's game, you can create situations where you stand a better chance of winning the point. To me, that's what tennis tactics are—creating the situations that make your opponent uncomfortable.

MANUEL ORANTES

PANCHO SEGURA, dressed in a salmon-colored warm-up suit and wearing aviator glasses, was just beginning to immerse himself in a match between two of the best senior players in the world: Torben Ulrich and Frank Sedgman. There was a vacant seat beside him on the viewing balcony of the indoor tennis facility at The Greenbrier, in White Sulphur Springs, Va., and I slipped into it.

"That's a terrible mistake," I heard Segura murmur. For a second I thought he was referring to my intrusion.

"Pardon me," I said.

"Torben's last shot," Segura whispered and shook his head in the manner of a neurologist studying the X-ray of a terminal patient. "He hit the approach shot with too much topspin. Ball hangs up. Gives Sedgey time to pass him. Approach shots should always be hit low with slice. Slice keeps the ball down. Harder to hit a good passing shot."

Segura and I had yet to be introduced, but had you seen the way he spoke, and the way I nodded, you would have assumed I was one of his pupils—a future Jimmy Connors, perhaps, absorbing wisdom from the master. I wondered if I should introduce myself, ask Segura if he minded my presence, but I never got the chance. Below us, Sedgman cracked a sharply angled volley winner from the service line. Segura clapped his thigh in approval. "G-R-E-A-T S-H-O-T," he exclaimed, extending each word two or three extra beats. "Great shot. I like a guy who can volley both ways, short and long. Not many guys can do that. Not many at all."

By now you may have gathered that Segura is no more your typical tennis spectator than Cézanne was your typical landscape painter. Not content to simply *watch* a match, or even comment on what he sees, Segura experiences a tennis match on a multiplicity of levels: as spectator, as coach, as tennis theoretician. The levels of these experiences, moreover, are forever shifting, often blending, like the dialogue in a Pirandello play. When Ulrich ripped a backhand return deep to Sedgman's forehand, Segura was simply an admiring fan. "Hell of a shot," he said. "Hell of a shot." But with his next breath he chastised Ulrich for not following the shot to the net. "Look, he should be at the net now, but he's not. No good."

Unaware that his every shot was being scrutinized from above, Ulrich won the point anyway, but Segura would not overlook the transgression. "When you hit a good shot like that, you have to come to net," he said with quiet urgency, leaning closer to me now with his hand close to his mouth—the better to underscore the confidence we were sharing. "For me, the four winning areas of the court are the two alleys, way behind the baseline, and up real close to the net. When you got the guy in any of these four areas, *you come to net.*" His eyes flashed to the court. "Like *now*," he said, as Ulrich pounded a crosscourt forehand deep to Sedgman's forehand corner. "See, he should move up with that speed of his. But he doesn't."

Sedgman, remarkably, got to the ball and drove a forehand down the line. Segura was ecstatic for a second, then grumbled as the ball landed three inches out. "He should have won that point. Sedge should have won the point. Torben hit a great shot, but he should have come to net. That's the crazy thing about this game. You can do the wrong thing and still win the point."

The Catch-22 of tennis is that you can do everything tactically correct and still lose the point. And you can do everything tactically *wrong* and still win the point.

A brief illustration. During a crucial point in a match against Ilie Nastase at Myrtle Beach, South Carolina, Manuel Orantes gradually worked Nastase out of court on the backhand side with a succession of looping forehands. Orantes knows Nastase's game as well as anyone can be expected to know the game of an unpredictable genius, and he was reasonably sure that if he got a short ball and went down the line to Nastase's forehand, Nastase, even with his speed, would not get to the ball soon enough to hit crosscourt. In all likelihood, he would go for broke down the line. So Orantes took a Nastase backhand that bounced short on the service and hit a picture-book forehand approach shot to the forehand corner. And, sure enough, the scurrying Nastase laced a passing shot down the line. Orantes could not have been in better position for the volley. He hit it into the net.

Invariably, during the press conferences that follow tournament matches, there will be questions regarding tactics, but the questions rarely make much sense—and the answers are even less frequently illuminating. The reason is that tennis, by its very nature, defies a nuts-and-bolts analysis. Not that there isn't a strategic logic to the game—enough that John Newcombe likes to compare elements of tennis to elements of chess.

Newcombe:

You're working with a lot of the same principles. Offense, defense, position—things like that. If you play too offensively, you leave yourself vulnerable. If you play too defensively, the only way you can win is if the other player makes the mistakes.

But the analogy only works to a point. There are indeed principles of tennis strategy that lend themselves to a reasonably scientific approach. You would like to ace Jimmy Connors? No problem. Sit down with a physicist or a mathematician and work out with pencil and paper just how hard you have to hit the ball and *where,* taking into account Connors's position on the court and how fast he reacts. Do this and you will get the ball by him every time. You could probably work out a formula.

There is only one problem. The physical and geometric laws that can be applied to tennis tactics will work agreeably in your behalf only if you do your share of the work. You have to be technically, and physically, able to accept the challenge. In chess, the question of whether you are physically able to execute a particular move never arises. In tennis, it is more than half the battle.

Leafing through instruction books or listening to professionals and commentators talk about tennis strategy doesn't always leave you with this impression. At most tennis camps, there are strategy sessions in which one of the teaching pros stands in front of the group with a blackboard and a piece of chalk, drawing diagrams. The fact that half the people in the group cannot hit the ball over the net three times is immaterial.

"What you want to do in doubles," the pro will say, "is get your first serve in—a nice, deep, spin serve to the backhand. You follow your serve to the net and hit your first volley crosscourt and low. That forces the other player to hit the ball up and gives your partner a chance to poach and win the point."

The group acknowledges the advice with a collective murmur of understanding. Invariably, a guy in an Oleg Cassini outfit who has yet to hit a successful volley in his two-month tennis career asks, "Should you try to hit your volley to the guy's forehand or backhand?"

Books are not much better. The strategy sections of most tennis books have always struck me as being like

cookbooks written by cordon bleu chefs *for* cordon
bleu chefs. Oh, the assumptions: that the average
players can *get* 70% of their first serves in, or can direct the serve to the backhand or forehand at will; that
average players can hit their approach shots with
underspin, or their passing shots with topspin. When
the writer of a cookbook tells me, almost offhandedly,
to put in a cup of some ingredient I have never heard
of, I am tempted to burn the book. And when a tennis
professional tells a group of beginners that the best
way to deal with an opponent who is serving like gang
busters and coming to net is to "chip the ball low at his
feet," I am tempted to burn *him*. Doesn't he know that
not even Rod Laver can do that consistently? I'll take
Dennis Ralston's strategic advice any day: "Get the
ball over the net and keep it on the court."

Once a player has developed a certain degree of technical skill, *then* we can get out the blackboards, slide
rules, and calculators. But even among the professionals, tactical theories have their limitations. What
works against some players in some situations fails
against others in other situations. Lately there has been
a trend toward compiling statistics of a tennis match
the way they compile data for a baseball box score.
You can now find out what percentage of first serves
a player got in, how many points he won on placements
or on his opponent's errors, and so forth. Eventually, I
suppose, somebody will start keeping track of how
often a player bounces the ball before he serves, or
how much Pepsi he drinks between games.

Theoretically, this kind of information should give
us some tactical insight into a tennis match, but in
actuality it doesn't work out that way. In the Decem-

ber, 1975 issue of *World Tennis,* for instance, Saul Sigelschiffer compiled a chart containing a statistical breakdown of ten matches that took place in the 1975 U.S. Open at Forest Hills. The chart tells, for example, that in the Borg–Laver match, which Borg won in three straight sets, Laver hit twice as many winners, 55 to 27, as Borg, but he also made twice as many errors. Obviously, if Laver wants to beat Borg next time out, he should heed these statistics and cut down on those errors.

Except for one thing, and I'll let Laver explain it.

Laver:

When you play somebody like Borg, who is so fast and so dangerous on your passing shots, you have to put a little extra into your shots. And when you do that, you automatically reduce your safety margin.

What you have is physics and geometry on the one hand, and the human dimension on the other. Every tactical theory in tennis involves one or more of these three facets of the game, and every successful player has managed to incorporate into his game a tactical approach that suits both his physical capabilities and his temperament.

Jack Kramer:

For every "rule" you can make in tennis relating to tactics, there are dozens of exceptions. In the final analysis, the idea of the game is to keep the ball in play one more time than your opponent. How you do it is secondary. The best players are the

ones who can win points in a lot of different ways;
they can hit winners, force errors, outsteady the
other player, and, if necessary, outlast the other
guy. You always go out with some general strate-
gic plan in mind, but in a lot of matches it's mis-
hits and breaks that make the difference. It
sounds a little unfair, but that's the way it is.

On the court inside the Greenbrier tennis facility, Sedgman and Ulrich were smacking forehands at each
other with dizzying ferocity, the balls clearing the net
by inches. Segura was nodding. "Power," he was saying. "Real power. That's very good tennis, by the way.
Very good tennis."

I have read that groundstrokes are supposed to clear
the net by at least three feet. "Awful low shots," I said
to Segura.

"That's right," Segura said. "Gives you less time
to get ready. For me, that's good tennis. When you tell
me about Vilas and Borg and all those guys who hit
high—that's not good tennis to me. Those shots can
be cut off. You come in early and cut them off. That's
why Jimmy beats Borg all the time. He takes the topspin shot high and early. Hits it deep. Keep a guy deep
enough and there's no way he can pass you."

An image came into mind of a recent Borg–Laver
match at Forest Hills. I was thinking about the time
Laver drove Borg behind the baseline with a deep
forehand approach shot, and Borg uncranked a crosscourt passing shot with such topspin and at such an
angle that Laver couldn't even get his racquet on the
ball. "Topspin shots," John Newcombe says, "have
changed the geometry of tennis."

I mentioned this to Segura. Wasn't it true, I said, that a player like Borg, who can hit with such topspin, can make the net a very vulnerable place to be, even if he is deep behind the baseline? Segura knitted his brows and stared at me as if, for the first time, he was actually aware of my presence.

"B-U-L-L-S-H-E-E-T," he whispered, but without malice.

The lesson was over.

TACTICS: A HISTORICAL VIEW

IN the beginning, tennis was a leisurely, defensive sort of game—a contest, really, to see which player would miss a shot first. The idea that you could actually be an instrument in the miss was vaguely heretical, like wearing jeans to church. The very structure of the first tennis court, with the net narrower from end to end and higher than the net is today, was meant to minimize the effect of offensive attacking shots. When certain players began to generate offensive shots despite these obstacles, there was a move—unsuccessful—to make the net even higher. In particular, the serve was not considered an instrument of destruction. You used it simply to put the ball in play, careful not to exploit the fact that you were striking the first blow. It was all very civilized. Roscoe Tanner would have been banned.

It figured, given the Western temperament, that competitive players would grow weary of an exercise in which the main idea was to wait until the *other* player failed to execute. This impatience quickly manifested itself with the appearance of the first genuinely offensive shot in tennis—the volley struck close to the net. Volleys had always been legal, but the stroke was thought of mainly as something you hit in self-defense, when you were caught in no man's land and couldn't hit the ball on a bounce.

The person who changed all that was an iconoclast named Spencer Gore. Gore not only *moved in* but went so far as actually to *reach over* the other side of the net to angle away a return. (It was this practice of Gore's, incidentally, that led to the rule which now bans such incursions.) There is no telling how long Spencer Gore might have dominated tennis with his aggressive volleying had it not been for a racquets man from Harrow named Frank Hadow. Hadow was probably the first player to employ what was then—and still is today—the most effective defensive answer to the net charger: the lob. Using this technique, Hadow was able to force Gore to the back of the court repeatedly. Disheartened, Gore ended up losing in two long sets, 7–5, 7–5.

No wonder. Gore, silly guy, didn't have an overhead. And why should he? Necessity is the mother of invention, and the lob had not yet been born. It wasn't long, however, before it had replaced the volley as the game's major new weapon—that is, until the overhead came along and became standard issue in the arsenal of the attacking player.

The advent of the overhead restored to the offensive player some of the advantages he enjoyed during the salad days of Spencer Gore, but it didn't settle the offense vs. defense issue. To this day, in fact, the central element in tennis strategy has to do with the relative merits of offensive and defensive tactics.

In 1915, J. Parmley Paret wrote in a book called *Methods and Players of Modern Lawn Tennis:*

> *Could a perfect volleyer beat a perfect baseline player? An academic question. It's invariably a question of relative skill, not relative methods of play. There is no doubt that a judicious combination of the two styles will beat either one alone.*

And in 1976, Pancho Segura said: "If you want to win in today's game, you have to be able to play the whole bleeping court."

TACTICS AND GEOMETRY

BECAUSE it is played within an arena of fixed boundaries, tennis lends itself, theoretically, at least, to certain geometric principles—principles that have not changed essentially since the early days of the game. I quote again from J. Parmley Paret:

> *The intelligent student of the game becomes as familiar with the possibilities of the different positions as a chess player with the different variations of the opening and other familiar groupings of pieces.*

Position is the bedrock of tennis theory. Where you happen to be standing on the court when you hit the ball, and where your opponent happens to be—these are the two factors that will most determine how hard you should hit the ball, what sort of spin you put on it, and what target you aim at. With enough control of your strokes, and with enough understanding of the dynamics of court position, you can own the tennis world.

Suzanne Lenglen is a case in point. The leggy, charismatic Frenchwoman was essentially a pusher, but she could put the ball on a dime—literally—and she invariably positioned herself for her opponent's return so that she rarely had more than a step or two to move to reach the ball. She had a way of figuring out ahead of time the safest shots her opponents could make from certain places on the court. Anticipating these shots, she was comfortable in the knowledge that the only way her opponent could hit the ball away from her was to take a shot that carried with it a high risk factor. She gave her adversaries plenty of rope with which to hang themselves.

One of her contemporaries, Mary K. Browne, says in *Top Flite Tennis:*

> *Tennis critics are apt to dismiss Suzanne's marvelous ability always to be in position, waiting, by calling it uncanny anticipation and marvelous speed of foot. It is more than that. I maintain that other players have those qualities. I may say—I hope with modesty—that I myself have possessed anticipation and a good deal of fleetness, but I was never drilled from childhood in what the logical and almost invariable results of certain plays will be.*

Lenglen's strategic approach to tennis was based on a single premise: the destination of a shot was more important than the speed of the shot. In her mind at all times was an image of the tennis court in which a perimeter of court space, extending from the baseline and net five feet in, and extending from the sidelines three feet in, served as "vital" territory of her opponent's court. Somewhat farther in, extending about ten feet out from the center of the court in all directions, was another area of the court which she considered "no man's land."

As Lenglen saw it, any shot that didn't land in the "vital" area was a wasted shot, and any shot that landed in "no man's land" was a virtual gift to the other player. She would take a short ball and angle it sharply into the forehand corner, follow that shot with drives to the backhand corner and again to the forehand corner, and then chip a sharp, angled shot to the backhand side. This was just one of several sequences that gave her game a strategic complexity that very few players, to this day, have been able to develop.

It's difficult to say how effective a system like Lenglen's would be in today's game. The players didn't move quite so quickly in her day (how could they, with those outlandish outfits?), the balls were slower, and most players didn't hit with as much pace or variety as they do today. Had Lenglen ever confronted the likes of Billie Jean King, it's unlikely that her theories would have been as effective.

John Newcombe:

If a player is quick enough and has enough variety—it's very tough to commit yourself to a set position on the court. Take Nastase. On his backhand alone, he can do six different things and disguise the shot so well you never know until the ball comes off his racquet where it's going. The idea of anticipating the next shot on the basis of where you've hit your shot is fine, but only if the other player is cooperating.

René Lacoste, one of the fabled "Musketeers" of French tennis in the 1920s, carried a notebook with him to every match he played. Afterward, he would sit alone in his room and, like a scientist in the midst of a vast research project, record lengthy observations about the match and his opponent. Eventually, Lacoste developed an actual mathematical system of tennis—one that took into consideration the potential value of certain combinations of shots balanced against the margin of error. It also took into consideration the kinds of shots he had to hit in order to beat certain players.

One of Lacoste's frequent opponents was fellow Musketeer Jean Borotra, known as the "bounding Basque." Borotra was an unconventional but athletic player whose acrobatics at the net compensated for the fact that he couldn't hit the ball all that soundly off the ground. Few players have ever been harder to pass.

Lacoste went to his notebook. He deduced that the shot with the best mathematical chance of eluding Borotra was the quick offensive lob, taken on the rise, as Borotra was coming in. That shot struck the optimum balance between risk and potential success. It took Lacoste a while to learn the stroke, but once he had mastered it he gave Borotra fits.

"Of all the players in the game," Borotra later admitted, "the one player I fear more than any other—more than Tilden, even—is Lacoste. He kills me."

As you might imagine, Lacoste's system met its

toughest challenge in the person of Bill Tilden. The first time the two men played, in the challenge round of the Davis Cup competition in 1925, Lacoste made up his mind to change pace and direction on *every* ball, much as Arthur Ashe and Manuel Orantes did against Jimmy Connors in their Wimbledon and Forest Hills victories of 1975. For two sets, the tactics worked swimmingly. Tilden was getting caught out of position and was making uncharacteristic errors. At one stage in the third set, with a match point in his favor, Lacoste hit a ball that landed so close to the line it could have been called either way. Belatedly, the linesman called it out, and some people think that the late call took all the steam out of Lacoste. In any event, Tilden went on to win the match 3–6, 10–12, 8–6, 7–5, 6–2.

The pair met again a year later, in another Davis Cup battle, and this time Lacoste started out with a somewhat different strategic attack. He was hitting most shots right down the center of the court and mixing in some half lobs to Tilden's backhand. Years before, a so-called "center theory" of tennis had developed —the idea being that by keeping the ball in the center of the court you limited the amount of angle your opponent had to work with. The theory was employed mainly by net chargers, who recognized that if the baseliner tried for too much pace at too much of an angle the ball would go out. What happened, though, was that players who attacked down the center found themselves forced to volley back drives hit directly at them. The resultant defensive volley usually gave the baseliner a relatively easy passing shot the second time around.

In his second match with Tilden, however, Lacoste

was not coming to net. He would feed balls down the center, and when Tilden rifled an approach shot to the corner, Lacoste would counter with a quick lob to Tilden's backhand. Playing with a knee injury, Tilden had trouble adjusting to these tactics in the first set; but in the second set, he started to anticipate Lacoste's short balls soon enough and was hitting winners into the corners.

At this point, Lacoste changed gears entirely. Instead of hitting down the center, he began mixing sharply angled crosscourt shots with exceptionally high lobs. It paid off. "Lacoste's strokes were so exact and impenetrable," the defeated Tilden remarked later, "it made me want to crack him across the mouth with my racquet."

WORKING ON THE OTHER PLAYER

TO Suzanne Lenglen, tennis strategy was mainly a matter of hitting the ball to a certain place on the court and anticipating the likely return. To René Lacoste, tennis strategy was mainly a matter of figuring out which strokes worked best in which situations. Although there was a little of Lenglen and Lacoste in Bill Tilden, he was probably the first player to seize the confrontation aspect of tennis and construct a strategic framework around it.

"Never allow a player to play the game he prefers if you can possibly force him to play any other," Tilden wrote in his classic book, *Match Play and the Spin of the Ball.* "Never give a player a shot he likes to play."

With Tilden, the gentility and the curious aura of mutual cooperation that had pervaded tennis since its infancy went right out the window. More than anybody before him, Tilden saw tennis as more a mental and psychological struggle than a physical and tactical contest. If Lacoste's tactical philosophy was to build a better mousetrap than his opponent, Tilden's, in large part, was to find a way to put the other player's mousetrap out of commission.

George Lott, a contemporary of Tilden's:

Tilden was the greatest tactician in tennis history. He knew the weaknesses of every player and he was good enough to exploit them. The only times I ever beat him were when I was playing out of my head and he was having an off day. If he was having a "good" day, I might have just as well stayed home. If he was having just an average day, he could still get to my weaknesses enough to win the big points when he had to. And that was the thing. He knew—and you knew—that anytime he really needed a point badly, he could get to that weakness, so he really didn't have to work on it that much. Just being aware of how vulnerable you were to him put you under tremendous pressure.

Had Tilden wanted to, he could have intimidated players by virtue of his power alone. Yet, he often kept his big shots under wraps; he would seemingly prolong matches by playing to an opponent's strength. Some saw in this trait evidences of the frustrated showman in Tilden. Actually, it was the psychologist in him.

Tilden:

I would rather destroy my opponent's confidence by forcing him into error than by winning outright myself. Nothing destroys a man's confidence, breaks up his game, and ruins his fighting spirit like errors. The more shots he misses, the more he worries and, ultimately, the worse he plays. That is why so many are said to be "off their game" against me. I set out deliberately to put them off their game.

BASELINE ARTILLERY

IN retrospect, top-level tennis in the era immediately following Tilden's heyday seems to have been a succession of heavy artillery contests from the baseline. "Boom-boom" tennis. The best players of the decade—Vines, Perry, Crawford, Budge, and, later, Riggs—were essentially baseliners. With the exception of Riggs, there wasn't much in their tactical approach that warrants comparison with the positional emphasis of Lenglen, the mathematical complexity of Lacoste, or the psychological warfare of Tilden. It was the era of the slugger—Vines, in particular. "Vines could hit the forehand so hard," says Bobby Riggs, "that he didn't have to worry about position, or the other guy, or psychology."

Much the same can be said about Don Budge, whose strength, unlike Vines's, dwelled in his backhand. Budge says he never entered a match with any detailed strategic plan. He never even gave much thought to the weaknesses or strengths of his opponent.

Budge:

I played pretty much the same game no matter who my opponent was. I hit the ball hard and deep. If I got a short ball, I'd move in. Otherwise, I stayed back. I was in good shape so I didn't worry about getting tired. I didn't feel there was anybody who could outhit me. If I got behind, I'd generally hit the ball a little harder—put a little pressure on the guy's second serve.

A simple plan, and a devastatingly effective one. Witness what happened in the most famous match of Budge's career—his 1937 Davis Cup match with Baron Gottfried Von Cramm:

The key strategic decision I made in that match came when I was down, 2–4, with Cramm serving in the fifth set. The last thing I wanted was to go behind 2–5, so I figured I had to take a gamble. I made up my mind that anytime Cramm missed his first serve in the seventh game, I was going to move in, attack the second serve, and come to net behind it. Cramm had a high-kicking second serve that I could take on the rise with my back-hand, so I wasn't too worried about hitting it. But I needed Cramm to miss some first serves. I got lucky. Cramm had a consistent first serve, but in that game he missed his first serve—by inches —four different times and I won the point every time. It got me back into the match.

THE POWER GAME

AS equipment and players improved, tennis balls began traveling at a faster pace, and with this increased pace came a definite change in the strategic nature of the game. If you could hit the ball with enough pace, you cut down measurably on the amount of time your opponent had to prepare for the return. This, in turn, increased the likelihood of his making an error or hitting so weak a shot that you could win the point easily on the next return.

It seemed so sensible. Why go to all the trouble of moving your opponent around from end to end, or wasting your evenings working on mathematical formulas, or tinkering with psychology when you could reduce all of the strategic complexities of the game to one workable goal: *power*.

The "power game," or "the big game," as it's sometimes called, came to the fore in the early 1940s mainly because of Jack Kramer. Kramer was a rangy, athletic Californian who had been influenced in his youth by Ellsworth Vines, much as other kids his age had been influenced by Babe Ruth. Kramer, though, went a step further than Vines. Whereas Vines had been content to blast away from the baseline and wait until the other player either made an error or wilted under the pressure, Kramer felt it more strategically sensible to force the issue as quickly as possible. There was a pragmatism to Kramer that no other tennis player of note had ever shown. Why achieve in ten shots, he reasoned, what you could achieve in only two or three?

Kramer:

What a lot of people do not realize is that I was very much a percentage player. The basic idea of the "power game" was that you used the power in the most efficient way. I figured that the serve was the strongest offensive weapon in my game. As long as I was serving I had the advantage. So

why not take advantage of the advantage? Instead
of waiting four or five shots before coming to net,
why not come in behind the shot that you know
you can put the pressure on with?

Kramer didn't develop his power game theories entirely on his own. He had some help from a retired
automotive engineer named Clifton Roche. Roche is
best known for having developed fluid drive, but he
was also a tennis buff who recognized parallels between the principles of tennis and the principles of
engineering. Just as Lacoste had done years earlier,
Roche worked out a number of theories based on
geometry, but within a framework that was much
simpler. A typical Roche strategy had to do with shots
hit while running toward either sideline. Unless you
were going for a winner, Roche believed, you should
always go crosscourt. Why? Because the down-the-line
shot opened up too much of your court for the crosscourt return.

But there was a difference between what Kramer
and Roche were doing with geometry and what Lacoste
had done with it. The Americans were devising a
system that dealt with geometry on its own terms, and
the other player be hanged.

Kramer:

The whole idea of Roche's theories was to keep
things as uncomplicated as possible. I've always
felt—and I still do—that the less you have to think
about on a tennis court, the better off you are. I'm
not saying you don't go into a match with a plan
—you definitely should—but the plan must be
thought out ahead of time. Everybody who played
me knew that whenever I got a short ball to my

forehand, I was going to go down the line with it. So what if they did anticipate the shot—I figured that if I made my shot good enough and was in the right net position, it was going to take one hell of a shot to win the point. The percentages still favored me.

Not that Kramer altogether ignored the psychological element in power game tennis:

One of the big advantages of playing this type of tennis was that you could deal more effectively with the mental pressures of the game. The one thing I could do better than some players was to pace myself mentally as well as physically. Mostly, it was a matter of expending energy at the right times. Certain points in tennis are much more crucial than others. If you're on serve, or up a service break, and the score on the other guy's serve is 0–40, that point is not as crucial as, say, a deuce point or an ad point on your serve when there haven't been any breaks. You don't give that 0–40 point away, but you don't mentally press too much on it, either. If you waste all of your energy —mental and physical—on every point early in a match, you're not going to have that much left later on when you really need it.

Power Tennis. The basic idea behind it was to make the first offensive shot, then move to the net and pressure the other player into making the low percentage passing shot. The key to the system was a big serve. You didn't need a notebook or diagrams. You didn't have to worry all that much about your opponent's game.

You didn't even need a solid ground game. If you could pound your serve hard enough, move in fast and volley clearly, you had geometry and physics working on your side. There was very little your opponent could do about it.

Not that everybody could adopt this classic power game. It has never, for example, played a major role in women's tennis, although some players—Margaret Court, Virginia Wade, Rosemary Casals—have employed it well. "Most women don't serve hard enough or move quickly enough to play serve and volley—at least not enough to win consistently," explains Julie Anthony.

But in the men's ranks, it had an incredibly far-reaching effect, particularly among California-bred Americans and Australians. Look through the list of winners of the major tournaments from the late 1940s until the early 1970s, and you'll have trouble finding more than a handful of players who did not play some variation of the serve and volley game.

And in the early days of professional tennis, it was everything.

Bobby Riggs:

You had no choice. You were playing indoors on very fast surfaces and without great lighting. You had to get to the net before your opponent. I was a baseline player throughout my amateur career, but I had to learn how to serve and volley as a pro. Otherwise, I wouldn't have had a chance. Rosewall is another example. As an amateur, he was strictly a baseline player. The minute he got into the pros, and started playing guys like Gon-

*zales, he had to learn to serve and volley, too. He
never developed that strong a serve, but he had a
great volley and so it didn't matter that much.*

For obvious reasons, power tennis tactics were better suited for fast surfaces. Still, a number of serve and
volley players—Laver, Emerson, and Stolle among
them—won their share of clay court European championships, including the French, with serve and volley
tactics.

Roy Emerson:

*You weren't as effective with a serve and volley
game on clay as you were on grass, but I always
felt as though my game worked better on clay than
a clay-court player's game worked on grass. The
idea was still basically the same—to put enough
pressure on the other player so that he was forced
to make the good shot to beat you. A lot of European players who had grown up on clay weren't
used to that sort of pressure. They liked to have
more time to set up for their shots, but here you
had players like Mervyn Rose who were constantly
attacking and not giving them this time. After a
while it was the pressure that got to them. There's
a lot more pressure when you're defending than
when you're attacking.*

STRATEGY IN THE MODERN GAME

"ONE thing's for sure," John Newcombe was
saying one summer afternoon outside the pro shop of

the John Newcombe Tennis Center on Stratton Mountain, Vermont. "The game is a lot different today than it was four or five years ago."

There was a mildly pensive quality to Newcombe's statement, as though he were a royalist accepting the inevitability of socialism. Yes, the game *has* changed, and Newcombe, in a sense, has been one of the casualties. He understands the change—his is one of the most astute minds in the game—but like a number of other top players who were schooled in serve and volley tactics, he has not really made the adjustment.

Newcombe:

It's not just the slowing down of the surface. It's other things. Topspin is one. The speed of some players is another. The basic serve and volley tactics don't work any more. The whole idea of what was offense and what was defense is changing. Take players like Borg and Vilas. What they've done is to change the geometry of the court, literally. They can hit the ball hard and get angles at the same time. When you play against guys like that, the idea isn't to take the net—you try to bring them to the net.

Newcombe's view of the change in the tactical climate of tennis is not shared by a number of respected names in tennis—players mostly from the 1940s and 1950s who can't understand why anybody would have problems with players like Borg or Vilas, who hit a lot of shallow shots. "There's no way you can tell me," Tony Trabert once said, "that you can't attack a guy whose shots are consistently landing at the service line. I don't care what he's putting on the ball."

Trabert's sentiments are understandable. He is, after all, a *summa cum laude* alumnus of the power game school of tennis. But it's possible—just possible —that Trabert's prejudice in this regard cost the United States Davis Cup team a victory over Mexico in the 1976 North American Challenge Cup competition. For when the time came to choose between Brian Gottfried, a very solid, basic, serve and volley style player, and Harold Solomon, a gritty, tireless retriever who rarely charges the net, to share the singles duties with Jimmy Connors, Trabert picked Gottfried. Gottfried, he explained, had an excellent singles record against Raul Ramirez, the Mexican star, throughout the year.

Solomon saw it differently. "Tony," he said, "doesn't respect my game."

Well, if Trabert and other oldtimers do not respect the sort of tennis that players like Solomon, Borg, and Vilas play, the opponents of these players do.

Charlie Pasarell:

The difference between playing guys like Borg, Vilas, Solomon, or Dibbs and the baseline players who used to be in the game seven or eight years ago is that the new guys are so quick and so steady that, even if you get a short ball and come in behind it, you have to hit a very strong approach, and you have to make a very good volley. Otherwise, they'll get to the ball and hit it past you. The worst part is, you can't stay at the baseline with them, either. They're too steady. They hit with too much depth.

The rankings tell the story. In 1972, among the top ten players (as ranked by *Tennis* magazine) only one

—Manuel Orantes—could be considered a baseliner primarily. In 1976, the situation had changed so that only two out of the top ten players—Arthur Ashe and Dick Stockton—were *not* primarily baseliners. The slowing down of the surfaces is certainly one factor behind this change, but a bigger reason is that quickness, steadiness and topspin have shifted the percentages back to the baseliner and away from the net rusher. The pressure that used to fall upon the defending baseliner is now, in many instances, felt more keenly by the attacking player.

Moreover, the serve is no longer the weapon it once was. Service returns, on the whole, have gotten noticeably stronger. "That's where you see the biggest change," says Newcombe. "I don't remember a time when there were so many players who returned serve so well."

No one tactical theory dominates the professional game today. One group of players—Borg, Vilas, Solomon, and Dibbs—plays an essentially physical, retrieving sort of game. They come to the court armed with the reassuring knowledge that they are steadier, more patient, and more fit than the majority of the players they meet. They leave it up to their opponents to force the issue.

Borg:

I think the strongest part of my game is my running. I feel that I can get to just about any ball that my opponent hits and keep running and running and not get tired, so that I really don't worry about hitting winners. If the other player is making great shots, then I do something more, but usually if I can just keep the ball in play, I win.

Raul Ramirez is different. He is essentially an attacking player whose quickness and reach make up for the fact that he is not as technically sound as many of the players he faces. The main reason for his success, particularly in Davis Cup competition, is that he plays well under pressure.

Ramirez:

I never worry about getting tired, and when I go out to play, I always do so with the idea that I can win. I have different things that I'll do with different players, but mainly I concentrate on my serve and my return of serve, and I try to keep the other player always on the defensive. I found out that I don't have to hit that great an approach to come to net, because I can get to the net quickly and that puts pressure on my opponent to make a better passing shot.

Jimmy Connors is more of a traditionalist, almost out of the Don Budge mold.

Connors:

Sure I have an idea of what my opponent likes and doesn't like to do, but I tend to play pretty much the same game no matter who I'm playing. If the guy is hitting deep groundstrokes, I'll stay back and hit with him; but as soon as I get a short ball, I'm coming to net.

I should point out that Connors can afford to take a more aggressive approach against men like Borg and Vilas because, unlike most players today, he can take the topspin shot on the rise, thus forcing a player like Borg to hit his passing shots from deeper in the court than Borg prefers.

"There's a big difference," Connors says, "between a guy trying to pass you when he's a foot or so inside the baseline and when he's a couple of feet behind it. It gives you a little more time. And it gives him a little less safety margin."

Connors himself is one of the few players against whom opponents will make noticeable changes in their basic approach. This has been going on since Ashe beat him at Wimbledon in 1975 on the basis of a very carefully thought out, meticulously executed plan. It was developed by Dennis Ralston, Donald Dell, and Ashe himself and it was designed to deny Connors the one thing that had destroyed Roscoe Tanner in the semi-finals: pace. The idea was for Ashe to serve the left-handed Connors very wide to Connors's strength, his two-handed return. Dell explained the strategy later to Rudy Langlais, a *Village Voice* writer:

Connors has a great two-handed backhand shot, so in the deuce court we were trying to spin or slice the ball as wide as we could, conceding his good shot. Let him hit that shot all day long, because when you come in and hit your first volley, you're volleying into his weakness, his left-handed forehand.

Additionally, of course, Ashe did a lot of chipping and dinking, keeping the ball very low on his returns, forcing Connors to reach down for his backhand—a tricky business for a two-hander. Orantes did the same thing, more or less, when he beat Connors three months later at Forest Hills, and with similar success. The word quickly spread. The way to beat Connors was to "junk" him to death; to kill him with kindness, to serve him wide and volley to his forehand.

There's only one problem. Not many players can do that. Surprisingly few of the top players are much good when it comes to taking pace off the ball, especially the topspinners. And to play serve and volley to Connors's power—his backhand return—you have to serve exceptionally well or else get mauled by Connors's cannon-shot returns.

I watched Smith play Connors in the U.S. Pro Indoors, in Philadelphia, about four months after Connors had lost to Orantes at Forest Hills. Smith, a heady player, served Connors much as Ashe had served him at Wimbledon. On the first point of a game, or a 30–30 point, Smith would pull Connors wide in the deuce court and hit his volleys far to Connors's left. In between, he was firing bullets down the middle. For a set, at least, the strategy worked. Then Smith started to miss his first serves and Connors hit two or three winners off the wide backhand return. Before you knew it, Connors had won the second set and was up a break in the third. "The 'right' strategy," Smith said afterward rather philosophically, "doesn't mean anything unless you can pull it off."

Orantes made a similar discovery seven weeks later in Las Vegas. To say that Connors was better prepared for Orantes in Las Vegas than he was at Forest Hills is like saying that gambling is one of the attractions that helps draw visitors to Las Vegas. Connors's strategy was simple: to jump all over Orantes right from the start and not allow him to establish the tempo that had won Orantes the match at Forest Hills.

Orantes was out of the running after the first three games. In the press conference that followed, Connors was asked why he had run through Orantes with such ease, given the loss he'd suffered at Forest Hills. "Mainly," he answered, "it was just a matter of not letting him do what he likes to do."

Connors's statement sums up pretty much the basic tactic used by most of the top players today. The Ashe situation at Wimbledon notwithstanding, players do not generally go into matches with elaborate game plans.

Cliff Richey:

When you come down to it, tennis is a game of basics. If you're getting your first serve in, hitting the ball deep, and keeping the ball in play, there isn't too much the other guy is going to be able to do. When my father used to travel with me, people wondered about the signals he gave me. Everybody thought it was an intricate thing. Actually, he was telling me to calm down, or pick up my footwork, or pick up my mentality, or just get the bloody first serve in. It was that simple.

A few players will, of course, sit down ahead of time and plan out certain shot sequences. Ron Holmberg, as described earlier, used to sit down a half hour or so before a match and rehearse in his mind every tactical sequence he intended to carry out. But Holmberg was an exception to the rule. Instead of a master plan as such, most pros bring to the court a very general idea of what they're going to try to do and how they're going to prevent the other player from doing his thing.

Marty Riessen:

You always go into a match with a general idea of how the other guy can hurt you, and you try to fix on a couple of things. You think back to the last time you played someone and you try to figure out what went wrong—whether he beat you or you beat yourself. If he was beating you with better shots, it means you've got to figure out a way to pressure him more. So maybe you'll go in with the idea of attacking more than you usually do. If you beat yourself, you may think about just keeping the ball in play. But you have to keep it general because you never know once you get into a match how his strokes are going to be working and how your own strokes are going to work.

There are, as you might expect, "books" on most players. Nearly everybody knows that you have to keep on top of Orantes, prevent him from controlling the tempo. Nearly everybody knows that to beat Tanner, you must return his serve effectively—you can't let him relax too much when he's returning your serve. Nearly everybody knows that the way to beat Evonne Goolagong is to play patient, controlled tennis, and force her into errors. And as for beating Chris Evert, here's the formula Billie Jean King uses.

King:

You have to break up her rhythm, mix up your game a lot, get her somehow to start making errors so she doesn't put so much pressure on you.

But knowing *how* to beat a player and actually doing it are two different things. Mark Cox on playing Bjorn Borg:

I don't mean to sound like a defeatist, but I know ahead of time when I go out to play Borg that, with my sort of game, there's very little I can do to deal with his sort of game. The straight power game doesn't beat Borg. He's too quick and steady, and his passing shots are too good. To beat him, you have to play him the way Connors plays him: take the ball early and force him to hit passing shots from well behind the baseline, or draw him to the net, the way guys like Ashe or Orantes can sometimes do. I can't do either of those things, and I have to play too many perfect points to win games. There's tremendous pressure. The only way I have a chance is if I'm playing exceptionally well and he's having an off day.

Talk to women players about the way to play Chris Evert and you hear many of the same laments. You can draw up a game plan, but it usually doesn't do you much good.

Val Ziegenfuss:

When I first started to watch Chris play, I had the feeling that she wasn't as good as a lot of people were saying. I felt that if you could put pressure on her, you could get her to start making errors. The trouble is, when you put pressure on her, she hits a better shot. Her shots keep coming back and coming back so deep usually that you can't launch any kind of attack. Meanwhile, you know that if you make the mistake of hitting a weak shot in the middle of the court, she's going to move up and just put it away. I still think the best way to beat Chris is to try to beat her at her own game —to stay back with her and just slug it out. But the only player who can really do that effectively is Nancy Gunter—and Chris can usually wear even Nancy down.

From a strictly tactical point of view, the best players make tactical adjustments throughout a match— but in the upper reaches of tennis today such players are surprisingly rare. Among the top women players over the past few years, for instance, Billie Jean King is the only one who could play as well from the backcourt as she could at the net, and she was the only woman player who had the ability to genuinely exploit her opponent's weaknesses.

Among the men players, the number of so-called all-court players is on the wane, now that Laver, Rosewall, and Newcombe have eased out of the game. This leaves Connors and Nastase and, perhaps, Panatta and Gottfried as the only players in the top ten who can really pressure an opponent from both the baseline and the net. It isn't that other players don't have reasonable baseline or net games, it's simply that they can't hurt you as much in one area as they can in another. Whether Bjorn Borg, whose serve and volley tactics surprised everyone at Wimbledon, emerges as a true all-court player remains to be seen. If he does, and if he can stay fit, he should dominate tennis for the next ten years.

TAKING CHARGE

ARMED with less strategic options than the public is generally aware of, most professional players make an attempt early in the match to establish a tempo and a style that, in turn, prevents the other player from establishing his, or her, tempo and style. One hears a lot of talk about a certain player's "weakness," but that's a relative term. As Rod Laver once said of Ken Rosewall: "Everybody used to talk about Kenny's forehand as being his weakness. I can remember matches where his forehand hurt me as much as his backhand."

A "weakness," incidentally, doesn't necessarily have to be a stroke. A player who hasn't been training is frequently going to find himself engaged in long rallies whose purpose is nothing more than to wear him out. A player with a chronic injury will find some of his opponents not above extending points for no other reason than to pressure the injury. A player who has a reputation for choking on big points will find his opponent slowing down the pace on big points, tossing in those high easy loopers that are difficult to stroke if your elbow is slowly turning to steel.

Charlie Pasarell:

After a while you get to know which players are nervous on big points and which players aren't. Against certain players, if I'm receiving a 30–40 point on a second serve, I'll move a few steps over to the forehand side, let them know that I'm going to run around my backhand, and really pound the forehand. You do that to a guy like Newcombe or

Connors, and he'll blast the ball right down the middle for an ace. But other guys will get a little nervous or tentative. They'll either double fault or loop in an easy serve.

Striking changes in tactical approach are rarely seen in professional tennis matches, especially in close contests. Usually when a player makes a noticeable deviation from his basic tactical plan, it's too late to make a difference. There have been exceptions, of course. Fred Stolle took the French Championships in 1966 by deliberately slowing down the pace of his shots the better to exploit the fact that Roche, a younger player playing in his first big final, was nervous.

Stolle:

Tony missed a lot of backhands in that match mainly because he had so much time to miss them and so many places to which he could hit them. So he began to think and he changed his natural shot too often. I don't care who it is you are playing, if you get him to change a natural shot you have won a point, a very big point.

One of the most notable tactical shifts in recent memory took place during the 1963 final at Forest Hills, in which Rafael Osuna began waiting for Frank Froehling's serve ten feet or so behind the baseline and simply lobbed the ball back. I saw Arthur Ashe pull a variation of this tactic in a 1976 Aetna Cup match against Tony Roche.

Ashe:

It was Dennis Ralston's suggestion. I wasn't doing anything with Tony's serve at all. I couldn't handle the spin. Normally the best way to deal with that kind of a serve is to move in and chip it back, but I like to swing out on my returns, so Dennis had me stand five feet or so back and swing away. The returns made enough of a difference so that Tony's volleys weren't as sharp.

There is a feeling that professional players do not really "think" on the court as much as they simply "react" in certain pre-programmed ways. For some players, yes, but not for the heady ones. I once watched Bob Hewitt, one of the premier doubles players of the world, win a crucial point in a doubles match with a bold forehand, a down-the-line. When I asked him about it later, he smiled.

Hewitt:

Sure, I remember that shot, and you know something, I had it in my mind to hit it for three or four games. I saw that the net man kept inching over to the center every time I was served into my backhand. Now, in the pro game a down-the-line return is not really a percentage shot, because if you don't hit it well the net man is probably going to hit a winning volley; and if you try to make it too good, you're going to make an error. Still, I thought to myself, "If I get a ball that I can get to on my forehand, I'm going to go that way." I wasn't going to hit it so hard that I risked an error, but just hard enough so that even if the guy volleyed the ball, he wouldn't be able to hit a winner. You do that a lot in tennis. You notice a player doing something on a shot—maybe hanging back

*on a drop shot—and you make a little mental note
to take advantage of it the next time.*

But probably the most insightful description of tactical warfare I've ever heard in the professional tennis arena was given by John Newcombe, generally acknowledged by his peers to be one of the supreme tacticians in tennis.

Newcombe:

*There's so much more to it than having a plan, or
knowing a player's strengths and weaknesses. The
name of the game is pressure, and you can apply
it in any number of ways—by outhitting him, by
outthinking him, by outlasting him. You get a feel
early in a match for how your strokes are working and what the other guy is feeling, but you
don't want to tip your hand too soon. If I win a
couple of points in a row because a guy hits a
couple of loose backhands, I'd be silly to go after
the backhand again if I'm well ahead in the game.
You save up those opportunities, and when you
really need the point, that's when you go after
them.*

*Pacing is important, too. A lot of players concentrate and play so hard in the first set they burn
themselves out. So even if you lose the first set to
them, you're not really worried because you know
they can't keep up that kind of pressure for three
or more sets. That's why Laver won so many
matches after losing the first set. The other guy
was working so hard and concentrating so much
to beat him in the first set that Laver could walk
all over the poor guy in the next set. Then again,*

*when you're playing a great player—like a Laver
or a Rosewall or a Connors—that's what you have
to do: beat them mentally as well as physically.*

4

The Winning Edge

Basically, it's a very strong feeling that nothing is as important as winning itself. There's a big difference between wanting to play or to compete, and wanting to win. If you really want to win, you don't care how you look doing it, or what the other player thinks of you, or what the spectators are thinking. You make up your mind as to what you have to do to win and you don't let anything else interfere.

BILLY MARTIN

You reach a point when you start to understand who you are and accept it and then build your game around it. I was never a stroker. I didn't have the patience to go out and practice hitting thousands of balls. It just wasn't me. My game was built mainly around competitive desire. Winning was more important to me than looking good. I had weaknesses, but against most players, I could attack enough to keep them away from my weaknesses. But to play an attacking kind of

game, you have to be keyed up. Winning has to
mean a great deal to you.

VIC SEIXAS

S EVERAL years ago, I had a lengthy conversation with Clarence Mabry, the former coach of the Trinity University tennis team and now a business partner of John Newcombe's. We were in the large, western-style dining room of what was then known as the T-Bar-M Tennis Ranch, but is today called Newk's Tennis Ranch, and the subject of the conversation was *winning.*

Why is it, I wanted to know, that you can match two players who are just about head to head in every facet of the game—strokes, mobility, court savvy, concentration, and so forth—and yet wind up with one player winning nearly all the time? Mabry, a husky, square-boned man with an easy smile and a mellow Texas drawl, contemplated my question for a few seconds and said simply: "The will to win."

Don't worry. In no way was I prepared to let Mabry escape with so facile an answer. I recall a lengthy soliloquy in which I trotted out every 14-carat phrase in my psychology vocabulary—"Oedipal complex," "subconscious motivation," "aggression-guilt complex," you name it. I may even have introduced the question of prenatal influences, I'm not sure. What I am sure about was Clarence's response. He had nodded several times throughout my discourse, as though everything I was saying struck a responsive chord. But when I finished, he paused a moment and said: "Maybe. But I still say, it's the will to win."

The will to win. Here, to be sure, is one of those catchy little clichés that manages to say a lot without meaning anything—and mean a lot without saying anything. To discuss the phrase with athletes, coaches and psychologists is to become convinced that there does indeed exist a dimension to competition that transcends technique, strategy, concentration, and even the controlling of your nerves and emotions. But exactly what that dimension is, or how it works is something else.

"We used to pick players for our junior development programs in Spain on the basis of how they looked when they hit the ball," Andres Gimeno once told me. "Now we just have them play one another and pick the kids who win. You can teach a kid to play tennis easier than you can teach a kid how to win."

The logic is compelling, particularly if you view it in light of what other professionals have to say on the subject of winning. Rod Laver calls winning a habit—"something you don't really think about as long as you're doing it." John Newcombe once dropped off the tour for six weeks because, as he put it, "I'd forgotten how to win." Julie Heldman likes to make a distinction between players who play "to win," and players who play "not to lose." Torben Ulrich defines a champion as a player who has not only overcome the fear of losing but the fear of winning as well.

We have to be careful, of course, not to lose sight of the fact that the very nature of a player's game—his strengths and weaknesses—can often explain his performance against a player who seemingly holds an edge over him, or is thought of as a nemesis. Jack Kramer insists, for example, that the "edge" he supposedly had over the young Pancho Gonzales had less to do with psychology and more to do with the fact that he, Kramer, could hurt Gonzales more with his forehand than Gonzales could hurt Kramer with his serve. And Vic Seixas has a similar view about the characteristic way in which he and Tony Trabert used to perform against Ken Rosewall and Lew Hoad.

Seixas:

Some people were convinced that I had a psychological block when it came to Rosewall and that Tony had a block when it came to Hoad. It wasn't that at all. Rosewall was steady and precise enough that he could exploit my backhand, which Hoad could not do. I could attack Hoad, stay even with him until he'd have a loose game. As for Tony, he didn't have any real weaknesses that Rosewall could attack, but he couldn't deal as well as I could with Hoad's power. Okay, it can get psychological after a while. You start losing to a guy a few times and pretty soon you can get psyched. But if you can analyze the situation objectively, you can almost always find some logical reason for what's happening, and then try to do something about it.

Other situations come to mind. Arthur Ashe's surge to glory in 1975 was thought by many people to have come about because Arthur was finally able to overcome the "mental obstacles" that had kept him from winning big tournaments in the past. But Ashe's explanation was much less complicated. He'd trained harder in 1975, and benefited from the Supreme Court surface used in many of the tournaments he played. It didn't hurt, either, that three players who have historically given Ashe trouble—Laver, Newcombe, and Rosewall—were inactive that year.

Then there is the puzzling case of Stan Smith, whose sudden and prolonged slump, which began midway through 1973, is usually analyzed in psychological terms only. But surely it is more than coincidental that Smith's decline coincided with the maturation of numerous young pros: Ramirez, Connors, Borg, Vilas, Dibbs, Solomon, Amritraj, Orantes, et al. Smith, remember, is hardly the only world-class player whose career has been on the decline since 1973. What about Tom Gorman, Cliff Richey, and Charlie Pasarell?

You can't always measure this instinct in intensity of play, either. To have observed the way Chuck McKinley, a Wimbledon winner in the early 1960s, threw himself at shots that most players would have conceded as winners, was to have come away convinced that no one wanted to win as badly as McKinley. Yet people who know McKinley well suggest that McKinley was sometimes more interested in pleasing the crowd than he was in winning the match. "Chuck had a concentration problem, too," adds Billy Talbert. "If he'd hit a couple of good shots in a rally and they didn't win the point, he'd lose his patience and try for too big a shot."

But with all these reservations, it is patently obvious that some players bring to the tennis court a drive and intensity that go beyond technical ability and what we normally think of when we talk about "mental discipline." Mabry calls it "the will to win"; Billie Jean King describes it as "the ability to get 'em on the ropes and then *wham 'em*—now—and it's all over." And former Davis Cupper Allen Fox, who is also a psychologist, calls it the "killer instinct: the need to dominate, to prove yourself and build yourself by winning."

Whatever it is, certain players seem more possessed and driven by it than others. Tilden had it. So did Budge, Riggs, Kramer, Ted Schroeder, and Gonzales. But Frankie Kovacs apparently lacked it. According to Vic Braden, Kovacs was the only player he ever knew who could hit the ball hard enough from the baseline to make clean winners. And yet, according to Kramer, "If you could stay in with Kovacs long enough, sooner or later he'd figure out a way to lose."

Not so Bobby Riggs. If you talk about the ability to "win" among people who've been around the game for a long time, one name crops up more often than any other: Bobby Riggs. It is regrettable, but understandable, given the image that Riggs has cultivated over the past several years, that most people who never saw Riggs play in his prime do not appreciate just how talented a tennis player he really was. True, he was not beyond "accidentally" kicking a ball when he went over to pick it up, which gave him an extra few seconds to collect his breath, but Riggs did not become a champion because he had an inexhaustible supply of tricks up his sleeve. He was a very solid technician with a variety of games and the ability, as Billy Talbert describes it, "to bring into play on the crucial points the shots that would win, or force you into an error."

Riggs' explanation for this ability is basically that he learned at an early age to deal with the pressure of competition.

Riggs:

It was my upbringing, mainly. I had older brothers and we had a competitive household. Right from the start, whenever I was competing, there was always something at stake—winning was im-

portant. So after awhile I got to a point where I looked forward to the pressure because it always brought out the best in me. Sure, I had some nervous matches. I remember losing a couple of matches in Florida to Kovacs where I simply didn't play the big points well. But then when I analyzed the matches, I realized that I wasn't doing the right thing, wasn't going to the net enough. Playing well under pressure is one thing but if you're not using the right tactics, you're still going to lose. Okay, I had the nerves but I also knew what to do against every player.

And what about the Billie Jean King match?

Riggs:

It was mainly a case of overconfidence on my part. I overestimated myself. I underestimated Billie Jean's ability to meet the pressure. I let her pick the surface and the ball because I figured it wouldn't make any difference, that she would beat herself. Even when she won the first set, I wasn't worried. In fact, I tried to bet more money on myself. But I miscalculated. I ran out of gas. She started playing better and better. I started playing worse. I tried to slow up the game to keep her back but she kept the pressure on. No question, she played a great match, but I feel to this day that if she had given me a rematch the way she promised, I would have beaten her.

Like Bobby Riggs, Rod Laver had the advantage of growing up with older brothers in a competitive household so that competing under pressure was something that came early and naturally, but their basic approach to pressure was different. Laver lacked the tactical shrewdness of Riggs but made up for it with his daring: he didn't pull back on a big point, he usually hit the ball harder.

Laver:

It's hard to say exactly when I started playing that way but the way I looked at things I stood just as much of a chance of losing a point if I held back than if I'd go for broke. It definitely helped that I hit with a lot of topspin, but more than that it was a decision I'd already made about how I wanted to play the game. I would rather lose hitting the ball hard than win holding back.

Among the contemporary players who seem to radiate the "killer instinct" quality more than others, a few stand out. Jimmy Connors and Billie Jean King are certainly among them. Add John Newcombe, Cliff Richey, Raul Ramirez, and young Billy Martin. What is it about these players that differentiates them from, say, an Arthur Ashe or a Manuel Orantes or a Chris Evert? The answer seems to lie in their ability, at times, to make the force of their personality a factor in the outcome of the match. They can, as Bill Tilden once put it, "force the recognition of impending defeat on their opponents through the impact of their personalities."

Julie Heldman:

Some players have the ability to emotionally influence or dominate their opponents. This alone, without the equipment, isn't going to get you far; and if you've got enough equipment you can win a lot of matches without the emotional thing. But the really great player—a Billie Jean King, for instance—has both. She has the power to use the force of her personality in a match and she has the equipment to go along with it. I didn't have it. I think I learned how to use my ability well as a tennis player, but I was never able to develop the mentality of a killer.

We are trying to get a handle here on a quality that is extraordinarily elusive to define, even for the players who are most endowed with it. When asked about her idea of "killer instinct," Evonne Goolagong once told writer Candace Mayeron:

I don't even know what the killer instinct is. I suppose it's someone who wins love and love, who goes for every point. If that's it, then I don't have that. But I know that I would never give away a game to make my opponent feel better. I'd rather play a good player; it's awkward playing someone bad.

Billie Jean King herself sees it as a "mysterious thing"—the ability to be aware of, and relate to, an aspect of the competitive struggle that many other players are oblivious to. The first time I interviewed her many years ago, she talked about the difference between herself and Rosemary Casals.

King:

Rosie has never concerned herself with what I like to think of as the "higher levels" of the game. She goes out and tries as hard as any of us to win, and she doesn't choke any more or any less than the rest of us, but she doesn't seem to sense—maybe

she can't, and maybe she doesn't want to—the
psychological turning points in a match. She can
make the most spectacular shots, but not at the
right times. With me, it's different. I don't know
just what it is, but I become aware at certain times
in a match that now is the time to put on the pres-
sure. I can feel it, but I can't really explain it.

I once asked Pancho Gonzales about it. At first, he
discounted the idea that he brought to the court an
extra psychological dimension that made him a winner.
"I simply knew what I could and couldn't do," he said.
"And I knew what my opponents could and couldn't
do. I always played within myself."

Eventually though, when I pressed him, Gonzales
began to sound more like Billie Jean King.

Gonzales:

I can't say exactly what it was but sometimes I
could look across the court—especially if I was
playing Kenny Rosewall—and see something in
the other player's eyes that gave me a feeling he
was worried about double faulting. So I would
maybe shade over a little bit to my forehand on his
second serve, and a lot of times he would double
fault. I got to a point where I felt as if I had the
power almost to will the double fault.

Now we're getting somewhere. Vibrations on the
court—and I'm not talking now about the little gamesmanship "shticks" that go on sometimes, or the tirades
of Ilie Nastase—that escape the notice of the general
public but which sometimes go a long way toward af-
fecting the outcome of a match.

Consider, for instance, the look of disdainful disbelief that will often cross Billie Jean King's face when an opponent passes her at the net with an exceptionally good shot. Once in a while Billie Jean will do what Orantes or Tanner do in the same situation—grant the other player a gesture of appreciation—but more often the look that she fixes on her opponent in these situations is one that doesn't congratulate but rather hurls down a challenge to make the same shot again.

Julie Heldman:

Billie Jean can get you to take your mind off the match and start thinking about proving something to her. She can't do it with everybody. After a while she couldn't do it to me, and she never really was able to do it to Chris Evert. But there are a lot of girls who, to this day, are cowed the minute they go on the court with Billie Jean.

Not that Billie Jean is the only player who imposes this kind of psychic dominance. John Newcombe, after he has creamed your passing shot for a volley winner, will stay fixed at the net for a few seconds and address you with a glare that seems to say, "There, you bastard. I dare you to try *that* again."

Jimmy Connors, of course, has that girlish little finger wag, or the silly habit of puffing out his chest. Even so princely a fellow as Stan Smith, when he was winning, radiated a persona that some players found infuriating.

"You know the thing I can't stand about Smith?" Jimmy Connors said shortly after he turned pro. "It's the little smirk he gets on his face when he's ready to serve."

A few players carry the act *off* the court as well as

on. Pancho Gonzales was one of them. Vic Braden relates the following account concerning Gonzales's ri-
valry with Ken Rosewall on the pro tour.

Braden:

*As long as Gonzales was giving gas to Rosewall,
Gonzales would have nothing to do with him.
Nothing. But as soon as Rosewall would win a
match, the next morning you'd see Pancho having breakfast or something with Rosewall, just
friendly as hell. He'd soften him up, beat him, and
then have nothing to do with him again.*

The examples I've just cited do not fall under the
category of gamesmanship as we normally think of the
term. Indeed gamesmanship itself, while it is usually
talked about in terms of players who will "do anything
to win," is more often practiced by players who *lack* a
true winning instinct. Most of the men professionals
who know him well, for instance, will tell you that
Ilie Nastase's frequent flare-ups are not so much cal-
culated attempts to disrupt his opponent's concentration (although this is what usually happens) as they
are uncontrollable reactions to pressure. And oldtimers
say the same thing about Frank Kovacs and Art Larsen,
both of whom were capable of outrageous behavior on
the court (once when Kovacs was serving against a
player named Joe Hunt, he threw three balls up in the
air at once and drilled the middle one down the center
of the court for an ace; Larsen, whose war experiences
left an indelible mark on his personality, once played—
and lost—a set wearing a shirt that still had a shirt
hanger in it), but neither of whom was a "winner" in
the way the term is usually used.

No, we're not talking here about "tricks" or "psychs" as much as we're talking about generalized personality patterns. When Billie Jean King stares down an adversary who has just blasted a brilliant shot, she is expressing a genuinely felt emotion. She is like an imperial princess forced to defer to a chambermaid. Similarly, Gonzales will tell you that while he was competing against Rosewall on the pro tour, he had no special feelings for the man one way or the other. He didn't stay up nights scheming about what he might do to get under Rosewall's skin.

Julie Heldman:

That's the difference between players who really know how to dominate and players—like Nastase —who try but can't. You have to feel it. It has to be part of you, part of your personality. It's really a need to dominate, a feeling that because you deserve to be the winner, it doesn't really matter how you get the victory.

The idea of a player feeling as if he *deserves* to win is intriguing. Apparently, there are players who do not feel this as strongly as others.

Cliff Drysdale:

I can only speak for myself. Even though I always go out to win, I find that I'm often satisfied if I can just get by the first or second round. If I get into the semi-finals, like I did at Wimbledon one year, I think to myself, "Wow, isn't this super!" I'm not really thinking about getting any further. I'm not saying this is a good way to feel. But I was never really groomed to think of myself as a world-class champion. Maybe I have the ability and maybe I don't, but I'm very happy with the way my life has taken shape. Maybe that's the problem—I'm too satisfied with myself to really push myself further.

To certain players, winning takes on such significance that they will do *more* than the next player to achieve it. Alone, this drive won't make you a champion—not without the goods. Indeed, if the drive is *too* overwhelming, it may be self-destructive.

"It's hard to say which is worse," Ron Holmberg says. "Not wanting to win enough, or wanting it so bad that you don't have the patience or the discipline to do what is necessary."

One thing's for sure. The motivation to win is important not only for how it affects you at the time, but for how it affects you *off* the court as well—in the way of training, practice, and preparation. Even the mentally toughest of players—a John Newcombe for instance —admits that if he's not fit physically he can't summon the same mental resources he has at his disposal when he's in peak shape.

Cliff Richey:

The question of whether you win or lose a tennis match is often decided not on the court but the night before. It's when you decide between going to bed early or going out with the guys or with a girl for a few beers. If you're really committed to winning, the choice is made for you: you don't have to think about it. And if you have to think about it too much, it means that the match might not be as important to you as it once was. It's not an easy thing to control. Once I found myself hav-

*ing to make these decisions in my career, I began
to lose the feeling I once had on the court—that
every point was a war.*

Ted Schroeder, whose biggest asset was his competitive intensity, agrees. He likes to group players into
three categories.

Schroeder:

*You've got one group of tennis players with a lot
of talent but not much in the way of competitive
drive. You've got another group of players who
have tremendous drive but not much talent. Then
you have the third group—the players with the
talent and the drive. Those guys are the
champions.*

THE WINNING FORMULA

WHAT imbues some players with more of a winning drive than others? A lot of it certainly is cultural.
Australian Bob Howe once observed that as a group,
Americans and Australians tend to have more competitive drive than Europeans and South Americans.

Howe:

*I think this is mainly a question of the competitive
environment in each country. American and Australian players were motivated enough to learn
how to play—and win—on clay, but the European
players, as a group, never really learned to play on
grass.*

Personality and family background, too, play a telling part. It's hardly an accident that Cliff Richey and his sister Nancy Richey Gunter rank as two of the most competitive players in the game.

Nancy Richey:

My dad, who coached both of us, encouraged it. I started playing tennis before Cliff did and until he reached a point where he could beat me without any trouble, there was so much tension between us that we didn't even speak to each other off the court. What my father used to do was to set up matches between us that paralleled the pro circuit. One week, we'd be playing for the Italian Championships, the next week for the French Championships and then Wimbledon. He'd post the results on the bulletin board of the club where he was the pro, and there was tremendous interest among the members.

Sports sociologists have also long maintained that an affluent, psychologically stable family situation is not the ideal spawning ground for an athletic champion (or, for that matter, an actor or an artist). The reasoning here is that without a compelling need to attain a goal—be it financial or psychological—the average person will not be sufficiently motivated to devote the time needed to become a champion. It's interesting to note that while tennis has traditionally been an upper-class diversion, tennis champions, by and large, have emerged from middle, lower-middle, and, in some instances, lower-income backgrounds.

Julie Anthony:

Whatever the reason, some players simply have a greater psychological need to win. Winning takes on great meaning in and of itself. It is the catalyst to self-esteem. I think Billie Jean King is a good example. Billie always talks about the things she didn't have as a child. The struggle she went through to become a champion is very important to her. She's like a lot of players who cannot separate what happens to her on the court and off the court.

Other influences obviously help shape a player's competitive drive, some of them dwelling beneath the conscious level. The main point for now, though, is that the ability to *win*, which is not quite the same as the ability to *play well*, isn't one specific psychological entity that can be isolated and studied on its own. It's a generalized motivational state of mind that makes its presence felt more in certain players than in others. It's a state that can sometimes enhance, or sometimes disrupt a player's performance; it can also affect the same player differently on different days.

Billy Talbert:

I don't know exactly why, but there were certain tournaments and certain matches in my career where I was simply more motivated to win than at other times. I can't point to anything specific I did in these matches that was so different, except that I tended to play a little better. I was mentally tougher.

PLAYING NOT TO LOSE

ONE phrase you hear when tennis players discuss the psychology of winning (which, by the way, is not that often) is playing "not to lose." This is not the same as "playing to win," and should not be confused with "playing to lose." A player who is playing to win can lose, and a player who is playing not to lose can win.

Julie Heldman:

Most tennis players—don't play to win, they play not to lose. When you play not to lose, you go out and you do your best, but you don't go beyond that. You're not willing to put yourself on the line and do everything in your power to win.

Heldman adds that this pattern—"playing not to lose"—is particularly characteristic of women players:

The problem is that women in this country are not conditioned to exercise the kind of emotional domination that is often necessary on a tennis court if you want to win. Women are brought up to be cute and feminine, and so there is this conflict between what it takes to win and what it takes to carry an acceptable self-image. I could never do it. I could play well enough as long as my strokes were doing the job, but when it came down to me having to dominate the other person, I couldn't handle it. And that's what separates most women players from people like Billie Jean.

Psychiatrist Leon Tec describes the "playing not to lose" phenomenon as "fear of success," a phenomenon he explores in his insightful book, *The Fear of Success*.

Tec:

What many people identify as a fear of losing is really a subconscious fear of winning—a fear of not being able to cope with the responsibilities and the burdens. There is a little bit of this in all of us, and it will affect some people more than others and even when you recognize it in yourself, it isn't easy to change.

On the surface, the idea that success is harder to deal with than failure and that winning is psychologically less palatable than losing may seem like a contradiction. Not, however, if viewed within the context of Freudian thinking. In the Freudian scheme of things, any competitive situation resurrects stirrings of the Oedipal conflict—that is, the guilt associated with suppressed sexual desires toward a parent of the opposite sex, and with suppressed destruction fantasies of a parent of the same sex. As one tennis playing psychiatrist, Roy Whitman, puts it: "In the one-to-one combat of singles tennis, the victory is often equated with murder of the father, retaliation being expected internally or by the dying rival. This also holds true for daughters *vis-à-vis* their mothers." He adds that in instances where this guilt is too great or the destructive urges too strong, the result is sometimes a "complete inability to play."

In the Freudian view, any competitive activity presents a variation of the so-called aggression-guilt axis.

But tennis has its uniqueness. It is, remember, an individual sport (doubles notwithstanding). This means that if there is guilt attached to winning, it is all yours. You can't foist it off on any of your teammates. Secondly, in tennis—unlike, say, golf or track—the competition is *direct:* a veritable duel. In golf, you can avoid guilt by transferring the aggression you might feel toward your opponents to the course instead, and your superego will not mind. Golf, especially the prevailing medal-play format of competition, has a loophole to blunt the effect of the Oedipal conflict.

Tennis doesn't. It's difficult to get around the fact that to win in tennis, you have to defeat—i.e., destroy—the player on the other side of the net. And unless you can con the superego into making this act of destruction palatable, winning is not going to be psychologically easy for you (assuming, of course, you buy the Freudian line).

The situation isn't as bleak as it seems for there are a number of ways out of this psychological labyrinth. First, you don't necessarily have to *dominate* the other player in order to win. Ashe, for example, doesn't dominate in the sense that, say, Newcombe or Billie Jean King do, and neither does Orantes. When either of these players wins, it's usually because they are executing their strokes very well and working the game's strategic challenges to their advantage. Winning in this somewhat indirect manner helps get you off the hook with your superego. If the superego wants to know how you could have destroyed the other player, you can always throw the blame on the strokes. No jury would convict you.

Don't snicker.

John Newcombe on Manuel Orantes:

He's the sort of player—and there are a lot of play-ers like him—who plays his best when his game is flowing and everything is working for him. He's not really a grubber, like a Solomon or a Dibbs. It's almost as if, when he's not playing well, he doesn't feel as if he deserves to win.

But the problem with this sort of a displacement mechanism, as Newcombe points out, is that it doesn't work on days when your strokes simply aren't grooving. This might explain why the games of certain players will undergo an almost complete collapse on days when their strokes aren't working, whereas other players retain the ability to win in spite of off days. You see it in players like Raul Ramirez, who maintains you have to fight the impulse to be apologetic when bad shots win for you, or like John Newcombe, about whom Rod Laver once observed:

He's the sort of player who doesn't always look all that smooth on the court, and will sometimes even look bad on certain points. But he gets the job done. When he needs a big point, he has a way of getting it, no matter what the other player does.

Another way of displacing the guilt associated with winning apparently is to disengage your own rewards from victory and do it instead for somebody else— for Daddy, Mom's apple pie, the flag. For the Gipper. In the early part of 1975, when Chris Evert went through the only real slump she has ever had in her career, many people reasoned that Chris's problems on the court had something to do with her romance with Jimmy Connors. Chris had her own view.

Evert:

This was the first time I'd ever been really out on my own, with nobody in the stands rooting for me to win. All the while I was growing up, I never really won for myself—it was always for my mother or my father. Suddenly, when I had to win for myself, it was an entirely different thing. And that's what I had to learn. I had to learn to win for myself.

If throwing the onus of guilt on your strokes, or on somebody in your family, doesn't work for you, a seemingly endless variety of steps can be taken to help you deal more effectively with the responsibility of winning. Ken Rosewall, for instance, has a marvelous habit of hanging his head in despair even after he's made a super shot. Psychiatrist Arnold Beisser, who has written extensively about tennis, provides this explanation in an essay he calls, simply, "Tennis":

. . . several world-caliber players exhibit a consistently predictable kind of behavior when they are winning. They begin to castigate themselves. They speak to themselves critically, as to another person, with expressions such as, "You're terrible," "You're lousy," "You can't play." This is indeed surprising to hear after a player makes a brilliant shot. It is incongruous to see a player on one of his best days behaving in this way, especially when on a bad day he has no need to do so. It is a magical gesture in which the player denies his strength and potency. He says, in effect, "Look, I

am not really as strong as it appears. I am weak.
I am not winning as it appears, I am losing." By
this gesture, he hopes to avoid the retaliation
which unconsciously is certain to come to him if
he wins.

Interested in more options? How about making sure
that you don't win big. You eke out a victory instead
of overwhelming every opponent you play. Bobby
Riggs did this all the time. So did Rod Laver and John
Newcombe. Beisser, in fact, alludes to either Newcombe or Laver (he doesn't mention either player
specifically) when he talks about the *real* reason for
this behavior.

By never winning an easy match, he attempted to
deny his potency by always having the same nar-
row margin of victory. If he barely won, he dem-
onstrated that there was little difference between
him and his opponent. This served as an uncon-
scious protection. The punishment he had to face
would then be small or overlooked.

Yet another way that a player (in Beisser's view)
can solve the problem of "distinguishing between his
destructive fantasies and the competition in a tennis
match" is to place the blame on the officials or ballboys
or courtside photographers in the manner of, say, Ilie
Nastase. Doing so, Beisser points out, results in the displacement of destructive fantasies to a less threatening
object and allows you to compete successfully against
your opponents.

I am not a psychiatrist, nor do I hold any great brief
for psychiatry one way or another. All I've tried to do

here is flesh out some of the theories that psychiatrists use to explain what really happens on a tennis court. Most professional players are either oblivious to these considerations or, if they've heard about them, don't hold much stock in them. Mention Oedipal conflict to Roy Emerson or Fred Stolle and they will douse your head with a can of beer. On the other hand, most successful professional tennis players seem to have worked out in their own way whatever subconscious hang-ups they may have about winning or losing. They have, in other words, found an approach to the game that not only produces victory but does so in a way that is acceptable to their superegos.

I'm not suggesting here that you fire your tennis pro and immediately set aside $5,000 for a year of psychoanalysis. But I've pondered these concepts not only in relation to myself but to club and professional players I've come to know and watch and I have the following observations to offer. You make your own comments.

Item. The two winningest players in tennis right now—Jimmy Connors and Chris Evert—were each taught to play by a parent of the *opposite* sex: in Jimmy's case, his mother and grandmother; in Chris's case, her father. Don't ask me what this reversal of parent/mentor roles does *vis-à-vis* the Oedipal conflict, but in the view of many psychiatrists the amount of guilt that needs displacing is *less* in situations where the father figure is *not* a member of the same sex.

Item. There are many players who are much stronger in doubles than in singles. Part of the reason for this difference could be a player's age, his quickness or his style of game, but part of it could also be the difference in psychological environment in each game.

In doubles, the burden of winning—and losing—is *shared*, a fact that seems to benefit certain players.

Marty Riessen:

I'm a much better doubles player than a singles player and I'm convinced it's the team aspect of it. I played a lot of basketball when I was younger and I like the teamwork aspect of sports. Singles is a terribly individual sport. It's very lonely. You have no one else to share the victory with.

Item. No one group of players in tennis has ever won more tournaments in one era than the Australian players—Laver, Rosewall, Hoad, Emerson, Newcombe, Stolle, etc.—all of whom developed under the tightfisted influence of Harry Hopman. True, they were all good, hand-picked athletes who tended to train harder, as a group, than any other group of players. But I can direct you to a couple of psychiatrists who will tell you that the real reason behind Hopman's success was the strong sense of *team* feeling that the Australian players have toward one another, individual rivalries apart.

Tec:

It's very possible, that the ability of these players to think to themselves, "I'm not winning this for myself, I'm winning for Australia," goes a long way to ease the guilt they might feel if this weren't the case.

Item. Tennis players at all levels of the game, but particularly the professionals, seem to play their best when they are behind, and they have great difficulty closing out a match in which they are only marginally ahead. Just about every professional will tell you that the toughest game to win in tennis is the one in which you're serving at 5–4 or 6–5. Most people assume that this is because some people simply choke when victory is at hand, or they play "looser" when they're behind.

Tec:

The reason it's easier for some players to play so well when they are behind is that they do not experience the guilt conflict that comes with being close to victory.

Item. Up until 1975, Arthur Ashe was often stigmatized as a player who couldn't win big matches. Yet his Davis Cup record throughout this period was brilliant. Might this contradiction have something to do with the fact that Ashe, who is extremely patriotic, found it easier to win when he was playing less for himself and more for his country?

Item. Listen closely to what is said during and after a tennis match. You will hear guilt inferences that would promote mass neurosis in the Chinese army. The apology one player will frequently make to his opponent after a mishit has produced a winner is just one example. The characteristically self-effacing behavior of a winning player after a match ("Well, I had some lucky shots . . .") is another. "By denying your potency," Beisser reminds us, "you ease the guilt associated with domination."

Item. Viewed in a Freudian context, the "Inner Game" theories of Tim Gallwey may well be interpreted as the ultimate guilt displacement trip. Gallwey advises us to remove our conscious ego from the competitive process and to "let things happen" instead of making them happen. But a Freudian might point out that by doing so one is simply protecting the ego from the guilt of winning. You can't very well pin the blame on the ego if it wasn't at the scene of the crime.

Significantly enough, only one professional player who is winning championships today approaches the game in a manner roughly akin to what Gallwey advocates. He is Torben Ulrich, the current over-forty-five champion. Ulrich talks often of the challenge of the game as an experience in and of itself, quite apart from the implications of competition. But he was never a successful tournament competitor as a younger player and he is able to win as a senior not so much because of his mental approach, but more because he has continued to develop his strokes and is a remarkably well-conditioned athlete. Sven Davidson, the former Swedish Davis Cupper and a frequent doubles partner of Ulrich, considers himself a friend of Torben, but says nonetheless: "I understand very well the way Torben feels about tennis and his attitudes about winning, but I have told him many times that I don't believe it, that what I think he is doing is to give himself an excuse not to win."

If we start out with the premise that our ability to win is tied up with subconscious forces that took root long before we ever picked up a racquet, the logical question to ask is: "What can we do to turn a losing pattern into a winning groove?" The bad news is that there is no 25-cent solution. The good news is that an understanding of yourself coupled with a willingness to take certain steps, can sometimes change the pattern. The results may not be good enough to get you to Forest Hills, but they should certainly help to improve your tennis.

It seems fair to say that if a player is not tremendously motivated to win, he is unlikely to take the steps necessary to get into a winning groove. Arthur Ashe brought nothing new in the way of technical ability to the court when he had his great year in 1975, but he did approach that year with a greater sense of commitment than in years past.

Ashe:

It started in late December, when I got a look at the rankings, and saw that I was ranked the lowest I'd ever been ranked . . . way below guys that I knew I could beat. It got me mad. I made up my mind to work hard to change it.

It figures that the stronger you feel physically the easier it will be for you to dominate, or resist domination, on the court. But I never realized just how closely connected the so-called winning instinct is to a player's physical condition until I started talking to the pros about it.

Marty Riessen:

When you feel physically strong on the court, it carries over to your mental attitude. I know myself that when I've been training well and am in good shape, I'm much more confident. My whole game is more solid.

Martina Navratilova tells about the six weeks she took off in late 1974, during which she played very little tennis but instead worked several hours a day lifting weights and doing agility exercises.

Navratilova:

I was naturally stronger and quicker when I came back on the tour, but there was something else, too. It was a feeling I had when I went out for a match—that I really felt like winning and that I could win.

Roy Emerson:

Any time you walk on a tennis court in less than top physical shape, you're giving yourself a convenient reason for losing. Usually, that's what you'll do. When I was playing the circuit, I knew that there were players on the tour who had better strokes than I, but I had confidence in my body. I knew that I had trained harder and prepared myself better than the other guy, and I knew that if it came down to a fifth set, he was more likely to wilt than I was.

According to Freudian theory, the simple act of coming to the tennis court well prepared physically would undoubtedly qualify as an acceptable displacement for the guilt-aggression axis. If you win, blame it on your physical condition. And that, in the end, is what developing a true winning spirit is probably all about: coming up with ways of displacing subconscious guilt that do not decrease the chances of victory but enhance them. Training hard for a tennis match is obviously a more productive guilt displacement mechanism than some others we've been talking about. I can't think of a tennis champion in recent memory who didn't have tremendous stamina. It's easy to see what you gain: when you don't get tired, you don't make as many mistakes. But there is a psychological benefit, too. The fitter you are, the less you're going to have to struggle for points; and the easier it will be to dominate the other player without having to burden your superego with unnecessary guilt.

Does the superego really care how you displace the guilt? Probably not. If it did, you would hear about it. This is significant. The thing that most differentiates the players who have a true winning instinct is that they have managed somehow to displace whatever subconscious guilt the desire to win creates—and they do it in a way that does not inhibit their court performance.

Take Jimmy Connors, who is probably less affected by subconscious guilt than anybody in tennis today. A psychologist, Jay Weiss, has watched Connors play many times and marvels that he can generate such hostility and not be burdened with any guilt. His explanation is that Connors, like a lot of top athletes, has been raised from the cradle to believe that the world is a competitive jungle, a dog-eat-dog affair, in which only the fittest survive.

Jay Weiss:

He's the perfect war machine. Put him on a court and the guy on the other side of the net immediately becomes his enemy—a guy out to kill him. It's no wonder he doesn't have to worry about guilt. He's too busy protecting his hide.

From what I've seen of Connors off court, this theory makes sense. Except for Nastase, Connors has never been close to any player on the tour; in fact, for many years he had a minor war going with the American players—Smith, Van Dillen, Ashe, Lutz—who played Davis Cup. Not so coincidentally, Nastase is the only player who has been able to beat Connors with any degree of consistency over the past several years. Connors insists that when he went out on the court against Nastase when the two were friends, he didn't let their friendship interfere, but I have a feeling his superego doesn't go along with that idea.

A number of people—among them some of her sisters on the women's tour—see in Billie Jean King a level of hostility and aggression comparable to that of Connors's, but if this is true, Billie Jean has managed to handle these guilt-inducing forces in a fascinatingly effective manner. Unlike Connors (and Pancho Gonzales years ago), Billie Jean has never been a loner as such. To the contrary, she has catalyzed and symbolized the solidarity of the women's tour. But in doing this, she has also given herself one of the most psychologically accepted justifications for winning: a cause. In Freudian terms, a person who wins for a cause has an easy time displacing guilt because he can always insist that he didn't do it for himself, but for humanity, or whatever. Maybe it's a coincidence, but it wasn't too long after women's tennis had gained respectability (thanks in large part to her efforts) that Billie Jean abandoned that cause and took up another—World Team Tennis.

It seems safe to say that athletes who attain true championship status are, generally speaking, not models of psychological normality. (The same could be said, incidentally, for great artists, writers, and musicians.) Those tennis players who have been the most consistent winners over the years have brought to the court not only the tools needed to produce victory but a compelling reason beyond the surface rewards of the game (the money, the glory, etc.) for winning.

If I've created the impression that the winning edge or the will to win is a *negative* trait when observed outside the framework of a tennis court, I didn't intend to. Nor am I suggesting that the reason most people don't win more often at tennis is not because they don't play well enough, but because they're not aggressive or hostile or neurotic enough. Still, tennis is what Peter Bodo has called an "assassin's game." It's a duel with all the symbolic implications associated with dueling.

Psychologist Allen Fox, a man who has been there and ought to know, puts it this way:

Fox:

I don't believe that players play just for the esthetic satisfaction, for the thrill of hitting the ball right. Anybody who says that is kidding himself. That's just an exaggerated defense mechanism. Putting your foot on somebody's face is a very necessary part of winning a match.

ON BECOMING A HEALTHY KILLER

Is it possible to cultivate a winning instinct that won't riddle you with guilt—or worse, force you to displace guilt in a manner that disrupts the rest of your life? I can't really say, and I have talked to enough psychologists and psychiatrists to know that not many of them can say, either. How does one define "healthy" and "normal"? And by whose standards?

If there is a recommended model for cultivating

the winning instinct in a manner that is both socially and psychologically acceptable, consider the model exemplified by the Australian tennis players—particularly those who developed under Harry Hopman. Do not misunderstand. The Lavers, Rosewalls, Newcombes, Emersons, Stolles, Roches, et al. are not without their aggressiveness, hostility, and psychological quirks. Rosewall is distant and ungiving. Laver, when he was younger, was, by his own admission, "moody and difficult at times." And Newcombe generates an arrogance that has never endeared him to many of his fellow players.

But as a group, the Australian players have come to grips with winning in a way that can only be appreciated by getting a close look at how they prepare for tennis combat, how they engage in it, and how they react when it's over. The Australian players enjoy a sense of community no other group of players in tennis enjoys, with the possible exception of the American players (Smith, Ashe, Lutz, Pasarell, Ralston, et al.) who helped the U.S. dominate Davis Cup competition in the late 1960s and early 1970s.

You notice this most at practice sessions. The first time I ever watched the Aussies work out together, I was astonished to see Roy Emerson giving Ken Rosewall a lesson of sorts on how he might best return Stan Smith's serve. Ken Rosewall, remember, has one of the great returns of serve in tennis!

"Will Rosewall follow Emmo's advice?" I asked Laver later that day. "Probably not," Laver said. "But he'll listen. He doesn't want to hurt Emmo's feelings."

Rosewall lost that night to Smith and I was in the locker room when he trudged in. Being in the presence of a professional tennis player who has just lost a big match is like being at a funeral home: you never know quite what to say. Roy Emerson does. Seconds after the crestfallen Rosewall sat down on the bench and disgustedly began unlacing his sneakers, Emerson walked over and wrapped his huge arms around Rosewall's narrow shoulders. "Forget it, Muscles," he said. "You played a hell of a match. You'll get him next time."

I know what you're thinking. Cornball stuff. Except the Aussies really subscribe to it. In the spirit of rugby players, they believe in a simple credo which says, basically, that you work your bloody ass off in practice, fight like hell to win; and then, when it's over, you buy the bastard you beat, or who beat you, a couple of beers. Whether all the Australian players genuinely feel this way is secondary to the fact that they have been conditioned to *act* this way, and it seems to work. By allowing themselves a generous measure of guiltless joy in winning, they reduce the chances of having guilt affect the outcome of subsequent competitions. "We love to win," John Newcombe says, "and we're not afraid to lose."

I was also in the Aussie locker room a day later, shortly after John Newcombe had beaten Arthur Ashe. Newcombe trooped in first and was greeted with a predictably triumphant welcome. He was followed into the locker room by Fred Stolle, who was Newcombe's coach throughout the match. Fred Stolle is one of the most engaging men in tennis, and I thought it would be a nice touch to congratulate *him* for the victory, too.

"Nice coaching, Fred," I said.

Another player—Richard Nixon, perhaps—would have taken that opportunity to piously amend my compliment. Not Newcombe.

"Nice coaching, my bloody ass," Newcombe roared but with obvious good humor. "You want to know how good a coach he is? I'll tell you. Here I am, down a set to bloody Arthur, and not doing anything at all with the bastard's serve, and figuring to lose if I don't do something, and what the hell is Fred giving me in the way of advice? You better break him soon, Newk. You better break him soon. As if I had to be bloody bleeping told."

Leon Tec:

The difference between the Australians and the average player is that they have managed to convince themselves that winning, after all, is not a terrible thing and that terrible things will not happen to them if they beat the other player. It's something we should all try to do.

But there's still another dimension to winning on a tennis court that I haven't touched upon. I became aware of it during a lengthy conversation with Julie Anthony, who has always been a member of the supporting cast of fine women players. She says her status really bothered her until she found herself a few years ago as Billie Jean King's teammate in World Team Tennis:

Anthony:

Billie Jean is an incredibly forceful personality. She can be tremendously inspiring and she has a way of getting you to look at the world through her eyes. Mainly because of her, I went through a stage in my tennis where I became motivated to win and to do well more than ever before. I prac-

*ticed harder. I trained harder. Tennis became
more important in my life than anything else.*

But it didn't work out. Technically, Julie says, she
was never sounder, and she had never been in better
shape. Even so, she had a mediocre year:

*I simply wasn't comfortable with myself on the
tennis court. I would get mad and frustrated
with myself. I wasn't having any fun, and I was
playing worse than I'd ever played. I'd try to relax on the court. I'd keep saying to myself, "Relax,
relax, relax," but I just couldn't. Finally, I came to
a realization about myself. That I wasn't Billie
Jean, and that the important thing for me, per-
sonally, was not to become the greatest tennis
player in the world, but to enjoy each day without
trying to enforce something on myself.*

In retrospect, Julie says she's grateful for the experience, that it helped give her new insight into herself,
clarified the role of tennis in her life.

*All the time I was going to school and playing
tennis, I had the feeling that my schoolwork was
getting in the way. But now I realize that the
schoolwork was necessary in order to give me
the perspective I needed to really enjoy tennis
for what it was. When I first started practicing
with Billie Jean, I was convinced there was
something wrong with me, that winning or losing
had no impact on me as a person. What I realized
eventually is that the feeling you have about winning isn't something you can artificially create for
yourself. For some people—like Billie Jean—
winning is very important, an end in itself. And*

*that has to do with a lot of things that relate to
Billie Jean and her life. The question isn't whether
she's right or someone else is right. The question
is whether you can step out of your own skin and
try to view the world from somebody else's point
of view. I couldn't, and I'm very happy now that
I made this realization.*

THE WILL TO WIN REVISITED

WINNING, in the final analysis, is more an attitude than a result. One evening, after he'd "lost" a
match to a player who hadn't beaten him in years,
Torben Ulrich sat in a sauna inside the locker room
of the WCT World of Tennis in Texas and answered
questions. Having seen the match, I wanted to know
from Torben why he had chosen to stay at the baseline the entire match instead of attacking. Segura's
explanation earlier was that Torben was a masochist.
Ulrich has a different view.

Ulrich:

*If you already know before you play that if you
do a certain thing the score will be such and
such, then where is the challenge? The ultimate
in tennis is to play every player on his terms. So
today I thought I would try to stay back and not
play with the strategy that I knew could win. I
thought that I could stay back and not have to
come to net, and that sooner or later I could do
it. But I couldn't. And there was a stage in the*

match where something went wrong and it was
3–3 in the third set, and I thought to myself that
maybe I should change and go back to a strategy
that I knew would work. But then I thought, no,
that would not be the courageous thing to do. And
even if I did that—and had won—what would it
have meant? And so I lost, but it was exciting—
more exciting than if I had won the other way.

Vince Lombardi would have called it heresy, but let's not be too hasty in our judgment. Ulrich is doing more than paraphrasing what the old Grantland Rice saw about the game itself being more important than the outcome. What he's talking about, really, is growth and discovery—on or *off* the tennis court. Whether one chooses to view tennis within this framework is, of course, a matter of personal choice, but Ulrich, it seems to me, has more to say to club players on the subject of winning than all the strategists and all the "killers" combined. In his late forties and physically more fit than most of the players on the tour who are half his age, Ulrich is one of the great anomalies of tennis because his game has steadily *improved* as he's grown older, and it hasn't happened by accident. Most professional tennis players—and most club players, too, tend at a certain stage in their careers to decide that technically they've gone about as far as they can go. Ulrich has never reached this stage and probably never will. "Torben will be working on his game until he's eighty," observes one of his fellow seniors, Hugh Stewart. "The only trouble is that by the time he gets a complete game, he won't be able to move."

Perhaps. Ulrich, when he talks about life, frequently

uses the word "patterns," and constantly stresses the importance of establishing new patterns in life, the better to prevent inertia.

> *You bring these attitudes to anything in life. You set challenges—your own challenges—and you try to meet them, and that's the real struggle.*

I'm condensing here. Ulrich doesn't issue terse philosophical opinions. Most of the time, if you ask him a question, he'll answer it with another question, and you're never really sure whether he's confiding in you or pulling your leg. But viewed as a whole, there is to Ulrich's answers, as elliptical as they may seem, a view that is consistent and pervasive. It says, in essence, that the point of playing tennis is not really to win, but to approach the game in a way that, on the one hand, honors what Ulrich calls the tradition of the craft ("Doing it right") and on the other hand produces personal growth and discovery.

Slater:

> *You can only become very good at the game by honoring the craft of it. But maybe this is not enough. Maybe it's important, too, to take risks and be courageous—to see tennis in this way. There's always a balance between the craft and the individual, but it's always evolving.*

He means it. I once asked Jeff Borowiak what Torben says to him when he, Jeff, starts to miss shots and get down on himself in general.

Borowiak:

> *The one thing Torben keeps telling me over and over again is to relax and to never forget that I*

have the rest of my life—maybe sixty years or so—in order to achieve what I want to achieve in tennis. When you look at it in that perspective, winning and losing on one particular day just doesn't seem all that important.

Notes

The vast majority of the quoted material in *Tennis and the Mind* originated in personal interviews conducted by the author with the quoted people. Exceptions are noted below.

CHAPTER I

Sashi Menon's comments to Peter Bodo on page 39 are taken from Bodo's article on superstition in tennis, published in the April, 1977 issue of *Tennis* magazine. Tim Gallwey's ideas involving the role of the mind in tennis (pages 50–53, 56–60) can be further explored in his two books: *The Inner Game of Tennis* (New York: Random House, 1974) and *Inner Tennis* (New York: Random House, 1977). *Zen in the Art of Archery*, by Eugen Herrigel, was published in paperback by Vintage.

CHAPTER II

Harry Hopman's comments on choking on page 72 come from his book *Lobbing into the Sun* (Indianapolis: Bobbs-Merrill, 1975). Arthur Ashe's observation about choking comes from his *Portrait in Motion*, written with Frank Deford (Boston: Houghton Mifflin, 1975). The quote from Ted Solotaroff on page 78 comes from his article "Man against Man, with Civility," which appeared in the September 30, 1973 issue of the *New York Times Sunday Magazine*.

CHAPTER III

J. Parmley Paret's comments on tennis strategy on page 113 are taken from his book *Methods and Players of Modern Lawn Tennis* (New York: American Lawn Tennis, 1915). Mary K.

Browne's observation about Suzanne Lenglen on page 114 comes from her book, *Top Flite Tennis* (New York: American Sports Publishing Company, 1928). For more on Bill Tilden's views on tennis psychology see his classic book, *Match Play and the Spin of the Ball* (New York: Arno Press, 1972). Rudy Langlais' article on Arthur Ashe's victory at Wimbledon, page 131, appeared in the August 25, 1975 issue of the *Village Voice*.

CHAPTER IV

For a more detailed discussion of the "killer instinct" in tennis, see Peter Bodo's article on the subject in the November, 1976 issue of *Tennis* magazine. For more on Leon Tec's theories of the fear of success, see his book, *The Fear of Success* (Pleasant-ville, New York: Reader's Digest Press, 1976). Roy Whitman's observations on page 160 are from his essay, "Psychoanalytic Speculations about Play: Tennis—the Duel," which was published in the *Psychoanalytic Review*, Vol. 56, No. 2, 1969. Arnold Beisser's views on guilt displacement, page 163, in tennis can be explored further in his essay called "Tennis," published in *Play, Games and Sports* (Springfield, Ill.: Charles C Thomas, 1967).

Barry Tarshis is a thirty-eight-year-old free-lance writer who was born and grew up in Pittsburgh but now lives in Westport, Connecticut, with his wife, Karen, and his two school-age children Lauren and Andrew. A contributing editor to Tennis *magazine, his previous books include* The Asphalt Athlete, Julie Harris Speaks to Young Actors (*with Julie Harris*), Tennis for the Bloody Fun of it (*with Rod Laver and Roy Emerson*), Six Weeks to a Better Level of Tennis (*with Dennis Ralston*), The Steady Game (*with Manuel Orantes*), *and* What it Costs. *Mr. Tarshis's articles about tennis and other subjects have appeared in a number of national publications, among them* New York, Town and Country, Sports, Signature, Travel and Leisure, House and Garden, Womensports, *and* American Home.